£10-10
T 7/3

Library of
Davidson College

# INDIAN VILLAGE IN GUYANA

A STUDY OF CULTURAL CHANGE
AND ETHNIC IDENTITY

*MONOGRAPHS AND THEORETICAL STUDIES
IN SOCIOLOGY AND ANTHROPOLOGY
IN HONOUR OF NELS ANDERSON*

General Editor: *K. Ishwaran*

Publication 6

# INDIAN VILLAGE IN GUYANA
## A STUDY OF CULTURAL CHANGE AND ETHNIC IDENTITY

**MOHAMMAD A. RAUF**
California State University, U.S.A.

LEIDEN
E. J. BRILL
1974

*ADVISORY COMMITTEE*

J. Ch'en, (York University, Toronto, Canada)
P. C. W. Gutkind, (McGill University, Montreal, Canada)
J. O'Neill, (York University, Toronto, Canada)

Minda A. Bojin (Editorial Assistant)

ISBN 90 04 03864 7

*Copyright 1974 by E. J. Brill, Leiden, Netherlands*

*All rights reserved. No part of this book may be reproduced or translated in any form, by print, photoprint, microfilm, microfiche or any other means without written permission from the publisher.*

PRINTED IN THE NETHERLANDS

*In memory of my father*

# TABLE OF CONTENTS

| | |
|---|---|
| List of Tables | VIII |
| List of Illustrations | VIII |
| Foreword | IX |
| Preface | XIII |
| Acknowledgement | XIV |

I. Introduction . . . . . . . . . . . . . . . . . . . . . . . . . . 1
    Methodology . . . . . . . . . . . . . . . . . . . . . . . . 4

II. Caribbean Studies: Some Research Problems . . . . . . . . 8
    Foundation of the Plural Model . . . . . . . . . . . . . 11
    Unitary or Consensual Model . . . . . . . . . . . . . . 16

III. The Development of a Multi-Racial Society . . . . . . . . 20
    The British Occupation . . . . . . . . . . . . . . . . . . 22
    Summary . . . . . . . . . . . . . . . . . . . . . . . . . . 30

IV. Land, Peoples, and Cultures of Guyana . . . . . . . . . . 32
    Geographical Divisions . . . . . . . . . . . . . . . . . . 32
    Climate . . . . . . . . . . . . . . . . . . . . . . . . . . . 33
    Population . . . . . . . . . . . . . . . . . . . . . . . . . 34
    Administrative Structure . . . . . . . . . . . . . . . . . 38

V. The Village of Crabwood Creek . . . . . . . . . . . . . . . 41
    The Village Defined . . . . . . . . . . . . . . . . . . . . 42
    Georgetown to Crabwood Creek . . . . . . . . . . . . 45
    Growth and Formation of the Village . . . . . . . . . 45
    The Village Population . . . . . . . . . . . . . . . . . . 50
    The Village Setting . . . . . . . . . . . . . . . . . . . . . 56
    Houses . . . . . . . . . . . . . . . . . . . . . . . . . . . . 57
    Households . . . . . . . . . . . . . . . . . . . . . . . . . 59
    Household Hierarchy . . . . . . . . . . . . . . . . . . . 61
    Clothing . . . . . . . . . . . . . . . . . . . . . . . . . . . 63

VI. The Economy and Daily Life . . . . . . . . . . . . . . . . . 66
    Occupations . . . . . . . . . . . . . . . . . . . . . . . . . 66
    Rice Cultivation . . . . . . . . . . . . . . . . . . . . . . 70
    Annual Cycle of Rice Cultivation . . . . . . . . . . . . 71

VII. Social Organization and Symbolic Systems. . . . . . . . . . 75
    Family Structure. . . . . . . . . . . . . . . . . . . . . . 77
    Marriage . . . . . . . . . . . . . . . . . . . . . . . . . 79
    Caste System . . . . . . . . . . . . . . . . . . . . . . . 93

VIII. Religious Institutions: Concepts and Definitions . . . . . . . 97
    Hindus. . . . . . . . . . . . . . . . . . . . . . . . . . 97
    Muslims . . . . . . . . . . . . . . . . . . . . . . . . . 99
    Christians. . . . . . . . . . . . . . . . . . . . . . . . . 100
    The Role of Religions Among East Indians in Developing an Aggregate of Values . . . . . . . . . . . . . . . . . . . . 102
    Religious Festivals . . . . . . . . . . . . . . . . . . . . . 103

IX. Summary and Conclusions. . . . . . . . . . . . . . . . . 104

References . . . . . . . . . . . . . . . . . . . . . . . . . . 112
Index . . . . . . . . . . . . . . . . . . . . . . . . . . . . 117


## LIST OF TABLES

1. Plantations in Guyana by 1769. . . . . . . . . . . . . . . . . 21
2. Annual Rainfall Distribution . . . . . . . . . . . . . . . . . 34
3. Racial Composition of the Population (December 1964) . . . . . 35
4. Percentage Distribution of Racial Population 1911-1960 . . . . . 37
5. Inter-Censal Annual Rates of Increase, by Race, 1911-1960 (per cent per year) . . . . . . . . . . . . . . . . . . . . . . . . . . 37
6. Ethnic Population of Crabwood Creek. . . . . . . . . . . . . 51
7. East Indian Population by Generation. . . . . . . . . . . . . 51
8. Households by Number of Persons living in Households . . . . . 59
9. Houses by Number of Rooms . . . . . . . . . . . . . . . . 60
10. Household Types by Number of Persons . . . . . . . . . . . . 60
11. Average Expenditure and Income for a Plot of One Acre Yielding 20 Bags of Rice Paddy or 10 Bags of Processed Rice . . . . . . . 74


## LIST OF ILLUSTRATIONS

Figure 1. Map of Guyana . . . . . . . . . . . . . . . . . . . XVI
Figure 2. Plan of Corentyne District. . . . . . . . . . . . . . 43
Figure 3. Plan of Crabwood Creek . . . . . . . . . . . . . . 44

# FOREWORD

MOHAMMAD RAUF'S INDIAN VILLAGE IN GUYANA, is a welcome and significant contribution to Caribbean studies. It is more than a meticulously mapped ethnographic document. It is an empirical work that raises and seriously tackles genuinely theoretical issues. It is also a contribution to the growing volume of truly international sociological and anthropological literature that is being produced by non-western scholars trained in the social science techniques of the west. Thus, Rauf combines a high degree of professional competence in western techniques with a perspective that belongs to a non-western social milieu.

The importance of this monograph derives from several social factors. At the most visible level, this is the work of an anthropologist, belonging to an ancient, historical culture, who encounters fragments of it transplanted and transformed miles away from the parent culture. In other words, Rauf's study is essentially a study in cultural persistence and cultural change. The historical and contemporary situation of the East Indian community in Guyana provides him with an excellent opportunity to study such a theme. The Guyanese Indians went to the West Indies as indentured laborers where they were forced to cope with a new location, a new situation and a new history. Rauf addresses himself to the question of how they preserved as well as modified their original Indian culture. In the context of modern population shifts across cultural and geographical boundaries all over the world, a study such as this acquires special significance. It throws useful light on the problems of cultural survival and cultural adaptation.

In terms of theory, Rauf attempts to come to grips with an important contemporary sociological concept, not in abstract terms, but in terms of empirical, concrete and historical data. His study of the East Indians of Guyana is theoretically linked to the concept of cultural pluralism. Rauf not only offers a succinct account of the nature and limitations of this theory, including a critique of its most important exponent, M. G. Smith, but he also tests the theory against rigorously compiled empirical data. However, cultural pluralism is not merely a theoretical issue. It touches practical political policy at important points. Societies which had been held up as Western models of cultural and social integration of the highest order, and thus distinguished from culturally pluralistic non-western societies, have themselves been shown increasingly to be boiling cauldrons of ethnic conflict. This is true of the U.S.A., and critical sociologists are questioning the validity of the melting pot model. The British society, a byword for homogeneous, monolithic culture, is itself being threatened by Scottish or Welsh regionalism, and the recent influx of non-White population into that country has added yet another complicating dimension to the situation. Surely one can expect Rauf's study to clarify some aspects of such problems.

## I

As a student of Indian society and culture, I was particularly interested in the transformations and stabilities that seem to characterize Indian social and cultural systems under foreign conditions. Specifically, I was interested in the problem of the change-potential of the traditional Indian social system, whose continuity and stability in India have mesmerized its students, both Indian and foreign, to such an extent that they have tended to overlook its capacity for historical transformation. Rauf's study demonstrates clearly the inadequacy of the myth of unchanging Indian society and culture.

From Weber to Parsons, western sociologists have placed undue emphasis on the inwardness, exclusiveness and isolationalism of Indian culture and civilization. It is seldom realized that Indian culture and civilization have historically spread over the globe in ancient as well as modern periods. The case of the Guyana Indians is, of course, a modern one. What makes the case fascinating is the fact that the Indians who migrated to Guyana were among the most conservative element in the old country – the peasants from North India. Rauf's study shows that the Indian peasant is not inherently conservative, and that he can respond creatively to the challenges of new stiuations, taking advantage of new opportunities. No doubt he does tend to keep intact some of his cultural traits, but he knows how to survive under alien, often hostile, conditions.

The discovery confirms recent studies of Indian rural society, including my own of the Karnataka villages,[1] which show that the Indian peasant is responsive to change, and that he can be, and increasingly is, drawn into the process of modernization, and that he is getting himself meaningfully involved in modern social, cultural, political and economic structures. Therefore, this study substantially reinforces the validity of the continuity – in – change model of Indian rural sociology.

Rauf's account goes into deeper detail, and shows that the process of change has a clearly differential impact on different generations. To use the author's term, "the older generation", is more likely to preserve elements of old culture than the "younger generation". But this seems to be the case more in respect of cultural forms than their content. In other words, both generations tend to preserve the outward forms of their traditional culture more than its content, and the older generation does this more than the younger generation. Thus, essentially, both generations participate in a similar kind of process of cultural change and adaptation. It is one that emphasizes continuity in forms but leaves room for changes at the deeper level of content. This is a pattern that is not basically different from the pattern of change that obtains in modern India. Rauf's study, therefore, supports the continuity-in-change model of modernization as the one most adequate to explain the processes of social and cultural changes in most of the developing areas.

---

1. K. Ishwaran (ed), Change and Continuity in India's Villages, New York, Columbia University Press, 1971.
  ———, Tradition and Economy in Village India, London, Routledge and Kegan Paul, 1968.

In particular, I think this study has performed a very useful sociological task in liquidating the myth of the indestructibility of the Indian caste system. The model of change postulated in this study can pinpoint the areas in which the caste system can change and in which it can persist. Here, there are interesting details of the process that distinguish it from the similar process in India. In Guyana, endogamy is the aspect of caste that has disappeared, but in India it is the aspect that seems to be one of the most persistent aspects of the caste institution. But even in India, especially in the urban sector, there is a perceptible, but very slow, change taking place in this aspect of the system. In fact, the social mobilization process is forcing the caste system along broadly similar lines of change, even in India.

Apart from its value as a sociological comment on Indian cultural and social institutions or on Guyanese social structure, this study is of great relevance to the study of immigration in general. In short, it can be recommended as a contribution to that somewhat underdeveloped branch of sociology, the sociology of immigration.

## II

From the point of view of sociological theory, Rauf's work conceptually clarifies and empirically illuminates Smith's societal model of cultural pluralism. However, Rauf is quite critical of Smith's concept, and suggests a positive improvement on it by adding the historical dimension. He conceives of the pluralistic model, not as a static phenomenon, but as a changing, historical system. In this task, Rauf's background as a trained historian comes to his aid. I would recommend this approach as a healthy corrective to the epistemological rigidities imposed by a structural-functionalist framework. What I am suggesting, and what I find amply demonstrated in Rauf's work, is that the structural-functional approach is not necessarily opposed to the historical approach. Sociology and social anthropology would do well to get away from a sterile conflict between them, and explore the exciting possibilities of joining the two approaches in order to give us an understanding of social institutions and processes in depth.

Rauf contrasts the pluralistic model with the consensus model, and rightly associates the former with Smith and the latter with Parsons. In a very helpful general discussion of these models, Rauf notes the complexities inherent in both the models. For instance, he points out that the Smith model of plural society also contains the other model, but only in respect of the sub-units of society. I agree with Rauf's general proposition that the pluralistic model is analytically and empirically more useful than the Parsonian model, and that it can handle historically both systems based on homogeneous equilibrium and systems based on integrative stratification orders, that is, transitional as well as modern social systems.

Rauf's historical sense saves him from the structuralist fallacy of static dichotomies. He is alive to the historical possibility of systemic change from one stage to another. Indeed, he sees the East Indians of Guyana as involved in process of such a historical transformation. They are not only trying to preserve some of their traditional cultural traits, and thus strengthen the pluralistic model. They are also engaged in a process of adaptation, which involves a change in the direction of the Parsonian model.

The pluralistic model has generally suffered from being discussed in too abstract and theoretical terms. It is a merit of Rauf's work that he attempts seriously to apply the model to a specific historical case. Rauf has, I think, shown admirably that ethnicity and ethic conflict are characteristic of plural societies at a certain stage of their historical development and that as new generations stampede over their past, the pluralistic system might undergo a qualitative change. It may, however, be a long time before such a change can reach a significant level in Guyana. There is no doubt about the direction of the change.

Above all, Rauf presents his account as a simple community study. In this task, he has successfully combined the gift of scientific observation with the good historian's gift for vivid narration. The monograph is not only a scientific document, but it is also a readable and fascinating human document.

As a student of Indian rural sociology, I find it gratifying that Rauf's study demonstrates the existence of a substantial change-potential in Indian peasant culture, and that it was activated under the conditions obtaining in Guyana. Since this is a special case of such activation, it would be relevant to examine under what other conditions than transplantation that culture can become sharply dynamic. The patterns of change and adaptation manifested in the case of the East Indians of Guyana might prove to be paradigmatic of the present culture and society in India. In this connection, it may be urged that comparative studies of changes among the Guyanese Indians and changes in modern India should prove very revealing.

If nothing else, such a comparative study should go a considerable way in destroying the myths about a backward and stagnant rural Indian society. In the meanwhile, Rauf's study challenges us to reconsider many issues in at least two areas of the sociology of the developing societies —Indian rural sociology and cultural pluralism.

York University  
August 1973

K. Ishwaran

# PREFACE

DR. RAUF came to anthropology after beginning a promising career as a historian in his country. Having come to work for a Ph.D. at The Ohio State University in 1963, he found an appeal and a challenge in anthropology. He saw in it an approach to the problems of his culturally diversified country where he realized that anthropology was as yet unrepresented.

The present volume is the result of Dr. Rauf's field work among East Indians in Guyana. It deals with a familiar field of study, the acculturation and accommodation of a group of immigrants and their descendants to a new country. This is a subject which has particular meaning to Americans in this age of awakening ethnic consciousness. However, Dr. Rauf is able to provide a new slant on this familiar problem: the immigrants he studied, and more particularly, their descendants, are East Indians who migrated to Guyana. There they form somewhat more than half of the country's total population. The next largest group in the population are of Afro-American descent, while the remainder (Europeans, Orientals, Amerindians, mixed bloods) form less than 20 per cent. This process of acculturation and search for ethnic identity is one whose ingredients may be familiar to North Americans, yet the setting and the cultural elements of this potential melting pot are rather unfamiliar ones.

Again, while acculturation has often been studied, there is another novelty to be found in Dr. Rauf's work. It is not often that people, descendants of migrants, are studied by one who comes from the home country, one whose native culture is an intact version of the traditional culture of which the descendants of immigrants have only a dim and distant view. This personal background gave Dr. Rauf not only an excellent entry into the community and a position of respect within it. It also permitted him to measure, on the basis of his own knowledge, the cultural distance that had been traversed by the several generations of his hosts.

As so often happens in anthropological research and planning, serendipity intervened and the author was helped in this case by an unknown and fortuitous circumstance: the population to be studied was largely derived from that area of India in which Dr. Rauf had grown up and whose language was his own.

What we read in these pages, then, is not only a technical report by a trained observer. It is also the report of a visitor from the home country to its sons and daughters in an alien land, to which they have brought many of their own traditions and to which they have adapted, which they have helped to form by their work and by their presence, so that it is now in no small part a piece of the Indian subcontinent in the Western hemisphere.

It gives me great pleasure to be able to present his study to American readers.

The Ohio State University    Erika BOURGUIGNON

## ACKNOWLEDGEMENT

I WISH to acknowledge with gratitude my indebtedness to many people who made this study possible.

First, I would like to express my deep and enduring personal debt to Professor Leo A. Estel, who introduced me to the subject of anthropology. Since the time I entered the Department of Anthropology at Ohio State University, Columbus Ohio, he has been generous with his ideas, time, and advice. For the profound influence on the development of my ideas and knowledge in anthropology, I owe a great intellectual debt to Professor Erika Bourgiugnon. To acknowledge her help in this study is indeed an inadequate way of expressing my deep appreciation for sharing her learning and transmitting her scholarship. A special measure of appreciation must be expressed to Professor Edwin S. Hall, Jr., who spent many of his precious hours assisting me in many ways to improve this manuscript.

While preparing the manuscript I benefitted greatly from discussions with my friend and colleague, Professor Sharad Malelu, Department of Sociology, California State University, Sacramento. I owe a personal debt to him for providing me insights into many areas of this study.

A deep measure of gratitude is expressed to Professor Donna Jean Halstead, one of my former students and now a Colleague at California State University, Sacramento, who helped me in numerous ways in preparing this manuscript. I do not know how to give her my thanks.

Appreciation is extended to the United States Education Foundation (Fulbright-Hays Scholarship Program), which made it possible for me to visit and acquire knowledge in America, and to the Department of Anthropology, California State University, Sacramento, and Sacramento Anthropological Society, who provided me with every possible assistance in putting this manuscript into the present form.

It is impossible to articulate my expression in any way that can truly convey my feelings of appreciation and debt to hundreds of people of the village of Crabwood Creek who made many concessions so that I might live with them as a member of their community. I wish it were possible to name all of them here. However, I owe special thanks to Dr. Chedi Jagan, Mr. and Mrs. Mumtaz Khan, Mr. and Mrs. Mustafa Jamal, Mr. Ramnarain Matai, 'Maiyya' Matai, and Mr. Rabbani Ahmad. But for their help, patience, love and hospitality, the completion of this study would not have been possible.

Last but not least, I must express my appreciation to my wife Sayeeda, my daughter Seema, and my son Shariq. Their understanding and enthusiasm made the tedious process of writing this manuscript not only successful but also worth while.

The study which follows is a revision of my doctoral dissertation, "Crabwood Creek: A Study of Cultural Continuity and Ethnic Identity on Different Generational Levels Among East Indians in Guyana", Ohio State University, Columbus, Ohio, 1969, and my thanks are due to the Sacramento Anthropological Society which published the dissertation.

Sacramento, California  
November 1973

Mohammad A. Rauf

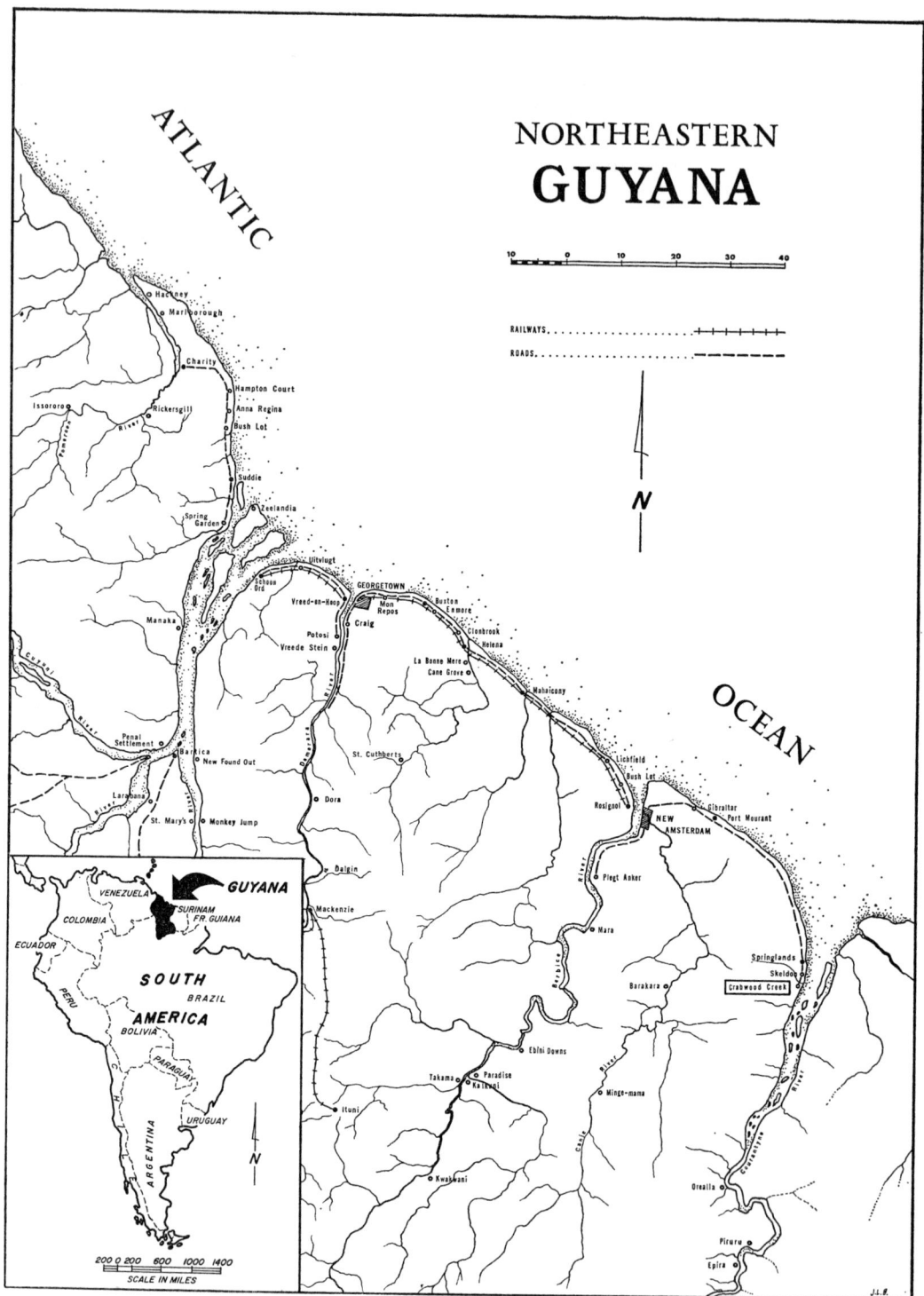

Fig. 1. Map of Guyana

CHAPTER ONE

# Introduction

THE PURPOSE of the present study is to examine and analyze cultural continuities and changes among a group of East Indians in British Guiana, a British "Sugar Plantation Colony" in South America. On May 26, 1966 this colony obtained its independence from British control and is now called by its newly assumed name, Guyana, a term which will henceforward be used in this study.

Guyana is often defined as a constituent part of the Caribbean area (Smith, M. G. 1965a: 21). By implication, therefore, a study done in this area is to be regarded as a study relating to the cultural region of the Caribbean. Scholarly interest in the field of Caribbean research has been frequently expressed either in the form of individual studies or through the regular research activities of various organizations and institutions such as University College of the West Indies, the University of Puerto Rico, and several other schools.

A major step was taken in the field, when in December 1956, the American Association for the Advancement of Science introduced a proposal to conduct a symposium on Caribbean Studies. The purpose of the symposium was to invite the attention of Caribbean scholars to the primary task of focusing their studies on the formulation of problems pertaining to the theory and methodology of research in the area, so that as a result of such initiative, further fruitful discussion might be stimulated among social scientists. The results of the symposium were published in 1957 (Rubin, 1960a). Two outstanding results were achieved: firstly, the symposium established the legitimacy of a dialogue between scholars interested in the study of the society and culture of the Caribbean area, and secondly, it revealed to the academic community that because many of the area's outstanding features, such as demographic patterns, specialized mode of economy, political history, geographical location, socio-cultural complexity and ethnic diversity, are directly observable within a set of small workable units, the Caribbean area is ideally suited for the development and the re-examination of various social scientific theories (Smith, M. G. 1965a: 19, 23).

The fact that the Caribbean was a relatively fresh area, not widely covered by social scientific research and field work, held a certain appeal for the investigator. What added more to the interest was the fact that among the various groups in the multi-ethnic society of the Caribbean, one of the constituent segments of the society is comprised of East Indians. This investigator belongs to this group by birth and cultural affiliation. Guyana stood out prominently over other units for having the largest number of East Indians in its population structure.

Before further elaboration of the problem, a brief account of some background information, which would place this East Indian segment of the population in proper context with reference to the other ethnic groups present in Guyanese society, seems to be in order.

The East Indians were brought into Guyana as indentured laborers as were workers of Portuguese and Chinese extraction. The manifest purpose behind their immigration was to fill the labor vacuum caused by the passage of The Act of Abolition (1834) which brought slavery to an end throughout the British Empire. After the dark period of slavery, the newly emancipated Negroes generally walked away from the plantations to enjoy the refreshing breeze of freedom in towns or in their own cooperative village settlements adjoining sugar estates. Under the changed conditions and their newly acquired status they worked on plantations as a task force on a job contract basis. Because of this mass exodus of former slaves, the newly arriving indentured laborers were placed in the rural areas and into the occupational category of agricultural laborers.

Implicit in the scheme of the indenture system was the motive to break the intransigence of the freed Negro laborers who refused to work on sugar estates on terms dictated by the planters. In the decades that followed the establishment of the indentured labor system in 1838, the planters pursued a deliberate policy of playing one group off against another. Mutual hostility and distrust were generated by employing cheap immigrant workers to undercut the wages of the emancipated Negroes, and racial distinction was engineered by dividing the plantation labor into two separate categories: "Factory Labor" (Negroes) and "Field Labor" (Indians). The Portuguese and Chinese immigrants could not long sustain the strenuous work in the cane fields and gradually left estate employment for urban areas such as Georgetown and New Amsterdam, where they established small commercial enterprises. Eventually, from among all the indentured immigrant groups, only the East Indians and a part of the freed Negro group were left as plantation workers.

Of itself, the presence of East Indians in Guyana as a part of the multi-ethnic society would not be of major consequence. The investigator's curiosity and research interest arose from the complexity of the social situation prevailing in the area in which six cultural segments of the society, namely, Whites, Portuguese, Negroes, Chinese, Amerindians and East Indians are found in constant interaction with each other. This research was undertaken to discover whether, in such a highly segmented society, the East Indian culture maintains sufficient unity to be recognized as a distinct socio-cultural unit or whether it permitted itself to be subsumed into the larger culture of the area.

The present study of East Indian society in a Guyanese village suggests the possibility of a re-examination of the notions of cultural continuity as found in anthropological literature. The study derives its primary significance from the situational context in which the group is placed. Nowhere except in the Caribbean area do we find a simultaneous exposure and contact of the East Indian group with five other cultural segments of the society; nor are there any other areas where East Indians lived in relative isolation without enjoying regular fertilizing contact with their resource culture. Thus, having attained its significance from the setting in which the East Indian culture is enmeshed, the study attempts to delineate other effective ways of talking about the continuities and changes in the culture. A survey of the anthropological literature on Indian cultural systems shows that the continuity and change within the Indian cultural system has been approached mainly in the following ways:

1. Some scholars have examined the premise that the continuity of the Indian culture may be looked upon primarily as the function of the continuity of the Indian social structure. Several anthropological studies of the Indian family structure and the caste system have suggested the validity of such assumptions (Berreman 1967; Srinivas 1956). The caste system has been regarded as being a "stabilizer of Indian society" and a sure means of "preserving the Hindu pattern of culture under the regime of alien conquerors" (Hutton 1951: 121; Dubois 1879: 82).

2. It has also been suggested that the continuity of the Indian cultural system can be explained not in terms of its structural continuity, but on the basis of its value system, ethos, the strength of its tradition and by "the common stock of mythological and legendary themes" (Brown 1966; Singer 1955).

The above propositions have been advanced, for the most part, on the basis of studies of the dynamics of Indian culture made within the geographical boundaries and social setting of the Indo-Pakistan subcontinent. The importance of such studies is beyond measure and they rightly deserve a position in the development of cultural theory. However, the observation of the East Indian culture as a part of the ongoing life in Guyana and a cognizance of the cultural posture that it is developing as one of the major components in the emerging society of this country, are suggestive of a new adjustment of the culture in an entirely different social milieu. As such it invites our attention to the fact that our approach to the examination of the notion of continuities and changes in Indian culture requires revision. It appears that when the carriers of a culture are placed in a set of controlled social environments which inhibit contact with their parent culture, and which generate constant interaction with other cultural segments of the society, the forces of change are likely to be more vehement and persuasive, and the culture is subjected to numerous pressures both internal and external. Consequently the present study addresses itself to the following questions:

Firstly, since the East Indians have now lived in Guyana in relative isolation from the main Indian population for a fairly long period, this study will examine whether their culture is largely a symbolic, ritualistic relic of the immigrant culture or whether it is an active, viable, and cohesive cultural alternative developing in the Guyanese social situation.

Secondly, the notion of cultural continuity will be examined with reference to the generational level. As the processes of change induced by the interactions with other cultural segments of the society are likely to modify the culture of the East Indian group, the problem of intergenerational differences in the retention of culture and in the interpretations of the cultural contents assumes legitimacy for investigation. It will be observed, therefore, whether the changes in the culture represent changes in the culture as a whole, or whether these changes have different social and personal meanings at the different generational levels within the East Indian community.

Thirdly, if for the purpose of clarifying possible research approaches we conditionally accept the theoretical position that Guyana is a plural society, it remains to be discovered whether the persistence of East Indian culture may be perceived as the function of the pluralistic nature of the Caribbean society or whether it should be treated as an attribute of the intrinsic vitality of the Indian culture.

Thus it is implied in the selection of the problem that the continuities and changes in the East Indian culture in Guyana are not intended to be examined by the simple process of recording a trait list and tracing continuity of the traits in terms of their form and structure during the period of East Indian existence as a part of Caribbean society. With the questions raised above, the study goes beyond the possibilities of simple narration of ethnographic data and a descriptive account of the Indian culture. Under these circumstances the study of the phenomena of continuity and change in the culture calls for a departure from the traditional descriptive approach to a productive analysis in a significant theoretical framework.

## Methodology

The present study is based on field-work conducted among a group of East Indians in Guyana during the year 1965 (June through October). The study of a culture, as a whole, involves application of a wide variety of techniques and methods that have been developed by anthropologists over time. Since the conceptual and logical orientations toward the study of culture have progressed with the growth of the discipline, it is natural that the need for adequate methods of investigation has also increased in proportion to the refinement of anthropological theory. Anthropological techniques and methods have grown as a result of experiences that anthropologists have gained in their field-work among the isolated tribes, peasant societies and, of late, among the urban dwellers living in slums and ghettoes of large industrial towns. This process is by no means complete. Every field investigation involves a unique experience and each human group possessed of different cultural contents and separate arrangement of its social relations presents new field situation to the anthropologist who seeks in his search to capture the wholeness of the culture. The ways in which a new field situation is handled and the experiences that are gained in the collection of the ethnographic data, when recorded, tend to enhance the possibilities of improvement in research techniques and methodology of the discipline. The shared field-work experiences today are, therefore, looked upon as one of the prominent sources of our methodology.

When I went to Guyana to do my field work among the East Indian group I found myself luckily placed in a favorable environment. An overwhelming majority of the East Indians of Guyana live in the rural areas where the social life is well integrated and the cost of living is low. It followed naturally that the ideal place for my research was a small village where the local cultural patterns could be easily observed. Since the study was financed by my own resources the obvious limitations of time and money did not prove to be a major obstacle under these circumstances.

To establish first contacts with the community is a matter of strategic importance in conducting field-work. The success of field-work largely depends on the sophistication of the community and the advance knowledge of the investigator. However, a slight negligence on the part of the investigator at this stage is likely to ruin his whole research project. My visit to Guyana followed almost immediately after the general elections in the country (December 1964). The after-effects of the election were noticeable in the form of tension in different political factions and racial hostility between the East Indians and the Guyanese of African origin. I had to take extreme care and precaution to see that the neutrality of my research would not be affected by the political and racial conflicts raging in the country. A young Pakistani gentleman who was a recent immigrant to Guyana and had married an educated East Indian girl of Guyanese origin provided great assistance to me in grasping a fairly objective picture of the local conditions. During the course of long friendly conversations with him, mostly in our own language (Urdu), I realized that being a recent immigrant he had not yet lost an outsider's view of the local East Indian culture and of the general social and political condition prevailing in the country. His help was also invaluable in establishing contact with leaders of all the ethnic communities and of different shades of public opinion. During these contacts I explained to each person the specific purpose of my research and sought for their help and cooperation. It was noted that frequently people would want to introduce local political issues as topics of conversation. On each occasion I held back my views by making a frank statement that such issues are not relevant to my focus of study. I later realized that this frankness eventually turned out to be an effective approach in establishing my credentials with all persons that I came in contact with during my field-work.

In the course of preliminary inquiries I was informed, as stated earlier, that most of the East Indians live in rural areas and also that the eastern part of the country (Berbice County) has generally a major concentration of the East Indian population. I planned an immediate visit to the area for my own assessment, keeping in mind the selection of a specific research site if the area was found as suitable as it was reported. After making a preliminary survey of the research possibilities and other facilities available in the area, I discovered that the village of Crabwood Creek was indeed suitable for my study. On returning to Georgetown I was pleased with my selection, when, during the course of a conversation, Dr. Chedi B. Jagan, a prestigious and one of the most well informed leaders of the country, suggested the same village for the study of the

East Indian community. My initial contact with Dr. Jagan was very useful. It dispelled doubts that might have otherwise arisen in the community by my constant presence in the village. After collecting necessary papers such as maps, reports of the Registrar General, copies of the Census Report and letters of introduction, I established my residence in the village and spent most of my time inside the village observing the general life style of the people as a participant in all social events and cultural activities.

Within a brief period of time I realized that I enjoyed a unique position in the field. Having been born in India I was looked upon by the community as a "honored guest" and "son of the sacred soil". I was accorded a warm reception in the village and was invited to all the local events and social functions. Thus the two major initial problems of field-work, entry into the group and establishment of rapport, were resolved.

It requires no emphasis that anthropological field-work is a deeply human experience as well as a scientific one. In passing through these phases of experience one of the most common problems a field-worker faces is that of maintaining a proper distance between himself and the people. This problem became somewhat delicate for me. I was viewed by the group as one who belonged to their own ethnic and cultural stock, and as such was allowed to move into the community quite freely. Because of this acceptance it became a trying job for me to maintain a reasonable distance from members of the community in order to meet the professional demands of objectivity. During the course of field-work I found myself always placed on the edge of a wave trying to balance between the human and scientific phases of the field-work experience. The acceptance by the group, in this case, did not prove to be an ideal situation. However, I handled this situation with the help of many informants, who, after the establishment of deeper relationship with me, felt free to offer objective information and their frank and critical opinion on many aspects of their culture. For the cross checking of the information and the collection of data a new device was adopted. It so happened that my membership in the teaching profession, involvement in field research in the village, and mode of living in the local peasant style became matters of curiosity and interest to a group of teachers in the local schools. Coincidentally during the time of field-work a teacher's training course was organized by the government in the same area. This scheme brought in more teachers from neighboring places and they formed a social group of their own for recreational purposes. For these teachers, the combination of my profession (teaching), field research in a village and the style of living like a peasant was a strange phenomenon. To satisfy their curiosity about me the teachers organized a social get-together and invited me as speaker to the group. I explained to them the purpose and the methods of my study and invited them, if they so desired to join in my research project. Their response to my invitation was extremely encouraging. Twelve teachers offered their help and cooperation. Their group consisted of members of both sexes and of all ages. I arranged for a regular meeting place where discussions were held on all topics in an informal atmosphere. After a brief period of time this discussion group turned into a research team. They helped me in almost every phase of my field-work: the collecting of the data; the processing of collected data; the checking and updating of the census report; the preparation of case histories and arranging interviews with the people. I assigned them various responsibilities from time to time which they carried out with sincerity and enthusiasm. The discussion hours were extremely productive. I asked their opinion first on the overt aspects of life—non-controversial questions about life routines, social environment, technical processes and every day attitude. Once they became relaxed in expressing their ideas I guided the discussions into controversial areas of their social and cultural life, and, after gaining some insights into the culture, I asked their frank appraisal of my own observations. Thus my contact with the group of teachers served several purposes: a) the reliability of the data gathered from the various informants was checked and counterchecked, b) new ideas were developed for further investigation, and c) with the team of workers involved, the whole village became interested in my research and volunteered any kind of information that was needed without reservations.

During the course of investigation all village activities such as weddings, funerals, ritual worship, festivals and all other celebrations were attended and a detailed account of daily routines was maintained. I used many available tools of social scientific research: participant observation, interviews, case histories, genealogies, census reports, records of the Local Authority and Sugar Estates, unpublished manuscripts, and original documents available in the office of the Immigration Agent General. Events were recorded with the help of camera and tape recorder whenever it was possible. Interviews with the people were held both in English and Hindustani. Conversation in the Hindustani language was a matter of delight both for me and the informants. They liked to hear me speak in Hindustani on many ceremonial occasions. Neighboring villages were visited intermittently. These visits helped me in comparing my notes and in perceiving the extra-insular relations that existed between the village and the outside communities.

Case histories and oral accounts of many first and second generation immigrants still living in and outside of the village provided time depth for the study. When the information elicited from the first and second generation immigrants was compared with the ethnographic data collected from the third and fourth generation of immigrants it brought forth meaningful insights. It was helpful first in determining original East Indian cultural patterns, and subsequently in recording the local interpretations of their social and cultural institutions, and in tracing progressive modifications in the arrangements of social relationships in the process of East Indian cultural adaptations to the environment of Guyana.

Toward the beginning of my study I had intended to use pseudonyms both for the locale of the study and for the informants. When I asked the members of the community and the informants, they expressed their desire that the actual names should be used. Thus, in deference to their wishes, the names of the places and of the people used in the study have not been changed.

CHAPTER TWO

# Caribbean Studies: Some Research Problems

THE CARIBBEAN AREA presents investigators with a complex social reality. It was at various stages in its history colonized by the English, French, Spanish, Dutch, Danish and Portuguese. These early colonists found relatively sparse native populations, a tropical climate, and rich soil which proved to be ideal for the production of sugar cane. Sugar plantations required a large labor force and, since the indigenous peoples "were soon decimated by disease, warfare, and slavery" (Wagley 1960: 5), the European colonists turned to Africa for slave labor. The plantation system, based on imported slave labor, gave a multi-racial and multi-cultural character to Caribbean society. This multi-racial, multi-cultural character became more complex when, after the abolition of the slave trade in 1808 and the abolition of slavery in 1834, plantation owners imported indentured labor from India, China, Indonesia and Portuguese Madeira to meet their labor requirements. Today the Caribbean area presents a complexity of variables. These include differences in national background, religion, and color; differences between the islands and the mainland; and differences resulting from the differential development in time of the plantation system (Wagley 1960: 5-12; Smith, M. G. 1965a: xiii, 6-17). Given this complexity it is not surprising that the study of this area has resulted in a parallel complexity of approaches and theories about the nature of Caribbean society.

The systematic study of the Caribbean societies is a relatively recent development. Research began with Martha Beckwith's studies of Jamaican life and folklore, published in 1929, and with an early visit of M. J. and F. S. Herskovits to Surinam. Herskovits and his wife conducted field work in Surinam, Trinidad, and Haiti, as well as on the West Coast of Africa. Out of their initial research came the first major theoretical approach to the area (Herskovits, M. J. 1937, 1960: 561; Herskovits, M. J. and F. S. 1934, 1947). Herskovits used an ethnohistorical approach which accounts for patterns of Negro culture in the Caribbean in relation to its African origin (Despres 1964: 1051). Based on his pioneering studies, a tradition of Afro-American research has developed which focuses on problems of differential intensities of Africanism in the economic, social, religious and aesthetic life of various cultures in the New World. The method employed in this research was the examination of the process of acculturation through studies of change or persistence of African cultural forms in the Caribbean area. The general goal of these studies was to gain insight into processes involved in acculturation (Smith, M. G. 1965a: 24).

Concomitant with this growth of an Afro-American research tradition, however, various other approaches have been utilized and followed. In its early stages Simey criticized the ethnohistorical approach on the grounds that it gave little insight into the dynamics of the present situation. Thus, he introduced a psychological approach in his description of a distinctive West Indian personality (Simey 1946). Both Kerr and Cohen have done further research in the area of culture and personality studies (Cohen 1954, 1956; Kerr 1952, 1955).

Redfield's approach to acculturation has also been used by some scholars in the Caribbean (Clarke 1953: 81-117; Beckwith 1929). This approach focuses on the social aspects of culture change, using the present as a base line, and analyzes social types in terms of their varying degrees of disorganization, secularization, and individuation when measured against his folk-urban continuum of acculturation (Redfield 1940: 731-42, 1947: 293-308).

Implicit in Simey's criticism of the ethnohistorical approach had been the idea of adaptive culture change. Julian Steward, in his studies of Puerto Rico utilized this idea within a "cultural evolution" framework. Steward advocates an "areal" approach to research. His model consists of a large complex social whole, areal or national, which is divided into three parts: vertical segments, horizontal segments and formal institutions. The social structure of this large "areal" whole is made up of the vertical segments, defined as local units such as communities, neighborhoods, and households, and the horizontal segments which cut across these local units and consist of occupational, class, caste, and ethnic distinctions which form sub-societies. The formal institutions, such as systems of trade, law, education and religion run through this total structure, "binding it together, and affecting it at every point" (Steward 1950: 21, 65, 115-16).

Students of the British Caribbean also utilized the idea of adaptive cultural change, but within a structural-functional framework. It is out of these structural-functional studies that the theoretical issues involving the plural model have arisen (Despres 1964: 1051-52). Structural-functional studies operate from a frame of reference which focuses on the interrelations of elements within a systemic whole. Historically this approach was made explicit by Radcliffe-Brown and Bronislaw Malinowski, upon whose work the British school of social anthropology is based. The approaches of these two men differ radically in some respects. Malinowski focused on culture, especially as expressed through institutions, and recognized each society as a highly integrated whole, the elements of which functioned to fulfill human needs. Radcliffe-Brown, following Durkheim, focused on society as the unit of study. He defined the function of the elements within the system in terms of the contribution made by each toward the maintenance of the social structure. (Radcliffe-Brown, again following Durkheim, and unlike Malinowski, did allow that some societies were less integrated than others.) Despite these differences between Malinowski and Radcliffe-Brown, the structural–functional school is oriented toward an approach which tends to assume consensus, and which emphasizes integration within holistic social systems (Keesing 1963: 150-155).

Investigators trained in the holistic, structural-functional tradition of social anthropology soon found that this approach did not prove "altogether adequate to the task of analyzing the more differentiated societies" of the Caribbean (Braithwaite 1960: 101). Problems arose in several different areas.

First, the complex reality of Caribbean society and culture was obviously bound up in its historical roots, but structural-functional anthropology had tended to avoid the historical approach (Beattie 1959: 121). Malinowski felt that research should be synchronic in order to avoid reconstruction or speculation (Smith, M. G. 1960: 34), and Radcliffe-Brown, although he felt that the historical and functional approaches supplement each other, also felt that since they were different kinds of explanation they should be kept separate, and, thus, he too avoided a diachronic approach (Radcliffe-Brown 1935: 400-401).

A second problem developed out of the observation that "analyses based on notions of system tend to avoid the problem of how a culture and a society are related," (Smith, M. G. 1965a: 78). The conflicting ideas of Malinowski and Radcliffe-Brown are perhaps part of the basis of this problem. Malinowski, following Tylor, saw society (social organization) as one dimension of culture (Smith, M. G. 1965a: 78), while Radcliffe-Brown saw culture as the activity and content dimension of social organization (Smith, M. G. 1960: 34-36). In an area as socially and culturally complex as the Caribbean, investigators have felt that the need for a clarification of the relationship between society and culture is vital (Smith, M. G. 1965a: 76-79; Braithwaite 1960: 101; Rubin 1960b: 785).

Thirdly, social anthropology has not been able to deal satisfactorily with the total social system of these complex Caribbean societies (Braithwaite 1960: 101-102). Implicit in the idea of functionalism is the assumption that societies are cohesive functioning units. Both Malinowski's concept of systems in equilibrium and Radcliffe-Brown's concept of function, which was borrowed from Durkheim, assumed internal consistency and unity (Radcliffe-Brown 1935: 394; Beattie 1959: 54). These assumptions did not seem to fit the nature of Caribbean societies with their complex cultural and social diversities (Braithwaite 1960: 101). M. G. Smith touches on the problem when he states that:

> It is obvious that when societies are conceived as structural systems in equilibrium, their homogeneity is assumed, and heterogeneity is difficult to define, classify, or analyze ... one general model, namely that of homogeneous structural systems, is applied to quite different types of society, thereby obscuring their differences, misleading their analysis, and blocking the development of social theory (1965a: 77).

Caribbean structural-functional investigators found themselves involved in basic problems dealing with the nature of social order, social integration, and social types (Smith, M. G. 1965a: vii). In searching for solutions they have borrowed models from other social sciences (Braithwaite 1960: 101). Among these investigators were M. G. Smith who borrowed a model developed by the British economist J. S. Furnivall and Raymond Smith who borrowed Parsons' unitary model from the field of sociology. Both of these models have attracted attention in the field of anthropology, and there is at present much conflict and debate over their validity and usefulness. The two models are based on mutually exclusive ideas. Parsons' action theory, with its unitary model, claims universality and assumes consensus in that it postulates (following Durkheim and Weber) that societies are integrated through shared values. Furnivall's model postulates that in colonial societies there is no consensus, and, thus, society must be held together by force imposed from the top (Smith, M. G. 1965a: vii-ix, 1965b: 1-8). Debate over the validity of these models finds expression in articles (Smith, R. T. 1961: 155-157; Despres 1964; Bryce-Laporte 1967 among others) and at conferences and symposia (Rubin 1960a, 1960b). Discussion and debate involving these two models are in turn a part of the general discussion and debate surrounding the various other Caribbean approaches previously discussed. Thus, in a very real sense, Caribbean studies today appear to be a microcosmic representation of the multiplicity of approaches and trends that together form the anthropological macrocosm.

## Foundation of the Plural Model

J. S. Furnivall, a British economist with many years of experience and study in Southeast Asia "was the first to distinguish the plural society as a separate form of society" (Smith M. G. 1965a: 75). The concept grew from his observations of the multi-racial, multi-cultural character of colonial societies in the tropics and from his study of Dutch colonial thought which recognized a "dual character of society" in both its political and economic theory (Furnivall 1944: 468). Furnivall had been trained in the tradition of Western political and economic theory, but in this Southeast Asian setting he found that his Western economic principles did not apply. Western theory took for granted the existence in each society of a common social "will", common social demands and a common desire for progress and welfare, however Furnivall found no such commonalities in Southeast Asian dependencies. Instead he found what he termed "plural" societies in which a "medley of people", usually European, Chinese, East-Indian, and indigenous native populations, "mix but do not combine" (Furnivall 1944, 1948).

> Each group holds by its own religion, its own culture and language, its own ideas and ways. As individuals they meet, but only in the market-place, in buying and selling. There is a plural society with different sections of the community living side by side, but separately, within the same political unit (Furnivall 1948: 304).

In plural societies Furnivall finds "no common will except, possibly in matters of supreme importance, such as resistance to aggression from outside" (Furnivall 1944: 447). Even in cases of defense against aggression, Furnivall warns that there may be apathy. He sees plural societies as being held together by force imposed upon the several sections by the colonial power, and he states that if this non-voluntary union were dissolved the result would be anarchy.

In terms of Furnivall's thesis true plural societies resulted from the impact of Western laissez-faire economy and political domination acting together upon tropical colonial dependencies. Western colonial powers tended to organize dependent societies for economic ends, with each section having its own function, and with an emphasis on production. According to Furnivall, not only was this a factor in the formation of the plural society, but also, and somewhat in contradiction, this resulted in internal disorganization within the separate units. Furnivall sees the growth of nationalism in each of the separate units as the reaction to this disorganization, and he sees nationalism as a destructive force in plural societies because it tends to set the individual sections against each other. He further felt that the basic problem facing tropical dependencies was to integrate the discrete sections and promote the growth of a "common will", and hence his practical proposals for action were oriented in this direction (Furnivall 1944: 446-450, 459, 463-468). Furnivall applied his concept to the United States and South Africa, and postulated a continuum of societies with varying degrees of plural character (Furnivall 1944: 446-447). In summary, Furnivall's model defines societies in terms of their political boundaries, and visualizes a plural society as made up of individual sections having no common will or wants, meeting only in the market-place, and held together only by force imposed from the top by an outside governmental power.

*Formulation of M. G. Smith's Model*: Furnivall's plural model was brought into the field of anthropology during the 1950's by M. G. Smith, an anthropologist born in Jamaica and educated in the tradition of British social anthropology. Smith conducted field-work in Africa among the Hausa, Kagora and Kadara (Nigeria), and in Jamaica, Grenada and Carriacou, in the Caribbean area. He began his studies of the Caribbean area by immersing himself in West Indian social history of the period between 1808, when the slave trade was abolished, and 1834, the year slavery itself was abolished. Working with historical material of the period, indexing and cross-checking the various accounts, he worked out an analytical reconstruction of the social structure of St. Vincent and Jamaica for the period "about" 1820. This gave Smith a base line "against which continuity and change could be identified and studied" (Smith, M. G. 1965a: xiii, 92). The results of the study indicated that the population of these colonies in the year 1820 fell into three distinct social sections—whites, free colored and free blacks, and slaves—and that each section differed from the other in kinship and mating patterns, family organization, education, religion, occupations, division of labor, value systems, folklore, and legal and political institutions. These results, which suggested a plural structure, coupled with Smith's personal experience in Grenada of strikes, arson, and general social conflict led him to consider Furnivall's concept of plural societies "defined by dissensus and pregnant with conflict ... (as) ... highly relevant to the West Indies" (Smith, M. G. 1965a: xiii, 112-113). Smith then undertook a systematic analysis of the extant historic and contemporary anthropological and sociological literature on the Caribbean area. He examined the major approaches that had developed in Caribbean studies: Afro-american studies, Folk-Urban theory, psychological approach, and stratification studies involving Parsons' model. Smith felt each of these approaches to be inadequate when used alone and sought for some way in which the competing models could be combined into an integrated theoretical framework. Again the answer seemed to lie in the direction of the plural concept (Smith, M. G. 1965a: ix-xiv, 18-74).

At this point in his thinking, Smith found himself going against traditional concepts which had their roots in the ideas of Emile Durkheim and Max Weber (Smith, M. G. 1965a: ix). Durkheim assumed that all societies possess a common conscience, a common sense of solidarity (Durkheim 1966: 226-229) and shared ideas about ends and means (Durkheim 1965: 492-493). For Durkheim, society consisted of these shared ideas, and thus, one of its organizing principles was the maintenance of consensus (Pitts 1961: 686). Max Weber also assumed that societies depend for their existence on a normative consensus. The alternative to this "willing submission" to authority was felt by both men to be a Hobbesian state of chaos (Smith, M. G. 1965a: ix-x). These ideas had entered anthropology through their influence on British social anthropology, and especially through Radcliffe-Brown who was strongly influenced by Durkheim (Keesing 1963: 153). They again entered the field through Talcott Parsons whose model assumed shared norms to be basic to all societies. Parsons' model was again borrowed by Raymond Smith and Lloyd Braithwaite. In opposition to these ideas, M. G. Smith, still looking on societies as single social systems and retaining the structural approach, raised the question as to whether complex societies were not in fact a different type of social system; a type in which the "willing-submission" (assumed to be necessary by Durkheim, Weber and those whom they had influenced) did not, in fact, exist (1965: x).

Turning to the plural model and using data from his Caribbean studies, Smith refined and developed Furnivall's framework and placed it within an expanded model which he felt could be used for the analysis of any type of society.

M. G. Smith defined societies as political units, stating that "only territorially distinct units having their own governmental institutions can be regarded as societies, or are in fact so regarded" (1965a: 79). He accepts Furnivall's basic model of plural societies as one distinct type of society, a type which contains separate cultural groups having few or no common values, and dependent for its existence upon force imposed from the top. Going beyond Furnivall, Smith defines the differences between the separate sub-groups of such a society in terms of differences between their respective institutions. For Smith, following Malinowski, institutional systems embody the core of a culture, since they involve "set forms of activity, grouping, rules, ideas, and values" (1965a: 79). From this it follows that differences or similarities in institutions produce differences or similarities in values, and a plural society is defined as one in which there exist sub-groups with different and incompatible institutional systems (Smith, M. G. 1965b: 4).

Smith further refines this concept by distinguishing between different kinds of institutions. Following Nadel he sets up three categories of institutions; "compulsory," "alternative," and "exclusive." "Compulsory" institutions are those basic institutions of kinship, education, religion, property and economy, recreation, and certain sodalities, which generally shape the life of an individual and which tend in general to be integrated into systems, with varying degrees of internal consistency and coherence. "Alternative" institutions are those which are shared by choice, such as class or community, and "exclusive" institutions are specialist categories such as occupational institutions (Smith, M. G. 1965a: 78-82).

Utilizing these institutional categories Smith presents a typology for the classification of societies. Societies are classed as "homogeneous," "heterogeneous," and "plural" on the basis of their differential sharing of the three institutional types. "Homogeneous" societies are those in which all share the same institutions. Most primitive societies would tend to fall in this category. "Heterogeneous" societies are those in which basic institutions are shared, but which also encompass differing alternate and exclusive institutions. Smith considers most modern societies, including the United States, to be heterogeneous. These societies often have plural characteristics and can sometimes contain isolated plural communities, but they share a common basic institutional system which sometimes varies in content, but not in form. "Plural" societies are those in which different groups of people, practicing different basic institutions, live within one political unit, and are held together as political units by governmental force imposed from the top by the dominant group. Smith considered Kenya, the Union of South Africa, Nigeria, and the complex societies of Southeast Asia and the Caribbean to be among plural societies. For Smith, such societies could not be stratified by class because class differences are "differences within a single institutional framework" (1965a: 82). In such societies class can only exist within the separate sub-units because only within these units is the common framework found within which judgments that are essential for comparison and ranking can be made. Within a plural society relations between the sub-units tend to be "specific, segmental, and governed by structural factors" (1965a: 81). Intersectional mobility within a given life span is seen as rare because it involves such drastic changes in institutional systems. However, Smith does state that in some cases "members of different cultural sections associate more regularly with one another than with the sections to which they belong ... [and that] ... in such cases the social and cultural sections have somewhat different boundaries, and their margins may be dynamic" (1966a: 82). While the preceding statement admits the possibility of peaceful interaction, in general Smith mentions competition and conflict as the processes of interaction between the sub-units (1965a: 88, 90-91, 151-54, 282-96, 318, 321). He states that because the plural society is dependent for its existence on governmental institutions imposed by the dominant group, "changes in the social structure presuppose political changes, and these usually have a violent form" (1965a: 91).

Smith's model is best summarized in his own words.

I have tried to show that the institutional system that forms the cultural core defines the social structure and value system of any given population. Thus populations that contain groups practicing different forms of institutional system exhibit a corresponding diversity of cultural, social, and ideational patterns. Since any institutional system tends toward internal integration and consistency, each of these differentiated groups will tend to form a closed socio-cultural unit. Such pluralistic conditions are far more widespread than are plural societies, the distinctive feature of which is their domination by a cultural minority. Pluralism is quite distinct from other forms of social heterogeneity, such as class stratification, in that it consists in the coexistence of incompatible institutional systems. Plural societies depend for their maintenance on the regulation of inter-sectional relations by one or another of the component cultural sections. When the dominant section is also a minority, the structural implications of cultural pluralism have their most extreme expression, and the dependence on regulation by force is greatest. A society whose members all share a single system of institutions is culturally and socially homgeneous. Since social integration develops institutionally, the structural conditions of societies vary according to their homogeneous, heterogeneous, or plural characters (1965a: 88).

Furnivall's model as revised by M. G. Smith introduces an additional dimension to societal analysis. Because of this dimension the model allows for the cultural analysis of complex societies in a way that the consensual models do not allow. The model focuses on institutional expressions of cultural values and, thus, points the way to differentiating between cultural patterns in complex societies through the measuring and comparison of values (Despres 1968: 15). While the model precludes the analysis of complex societies by models which assume consensus, it does not preclude the use of such models when applied to the sub-units of a plural society (Smith, M. G. 1965a: 83), or when applied to the analysis of homogeneous or heterogeneous societies. The model orients research toward problems of cohesion and calls for new structural models which can distinguish between social quiescence and cohesion, and between social regulation and integration. These differences cannot be distinguished under models which focus on society as the unit of study and/or which assume consensus and integration within a total social whole. In its recognition of the persistence of socio-cultural units through time, the model also makes a place for diachronic analysis in research (Smith, M. G. 1965a: xvi, 83, 90).

> Thus pluralism has three aspects of special significance for us: (1) on the theoretical plane, it directs attention to the need for refinement and variety of analytic models by presenting conditions that cannot be handled adequately with conventional models of homogeneous equilibrium systems or integrative stratification orders; (2) methodologically, there are the problems of studying such units holistically rather than in community segments, of classifying them structurally, and of assessing their relative integration in objective terms; and (3) analytically, the functional organization and development of such units also pose special problems that require historical study (Smith ,M. G. 1965a: 88).

It is difficult to assess the present position of M. G. Smith's model. Rubin lists it as one of the major conceptual approaches to Caribbean studies (1960a: viii). Braithwaite states that the concept has gained "fairly widespread adoption" (1960: 101), and Raymond Smith states that M. G. Smith's model has "provoked controversy as well as attracting followers; to the extent that there now exist "schools" of thought on the subject" (1966: 49).

Specifically, Smith's model has been criticized on the grounds that it "has no real dynamic dimension" (Smith, R. T. 1966: 49); that it is essentially pessimistic and deals only with a very limited range of conflict situations (Smith, R. T. 1966: 49); that it focuses on diversities but does not explain them (Braithwaite 1960: 101); that it reifies institutions (Smith, R. T. 1961: 156-57), Braithwaite in Rubin 1960b: 835-931); that Smith does not clearly define what he means by "conflict" and "competition" between the sections of a plural society (Bryce-Laporte 1967: 115-116); that in a plural society the model can only predict conflict "because the sections have nothing in common except involvement in economic and political relations which are essentially antagonistic" (Smith R. T. 1966: 49); that it distorts by explaining all conflict as rooted in a base of ethnic identity (Smith, R. T. 1966: 51); that it fails to adequately differentiate between plural and heterogeneous societies (Despres 1968: 12-13, Smith, R. T. 1961: 156-157); and finally, "the greatest amount of criticism... has been directed at Smith's view that there is no necessary functional integration of institutional systems or cultural sections at the societal level" (Despres 1968: 12).

## Unitary or Consensual Model

As was previously stated, the model's major rival in the area of Caribbean studies has been Parsons' theory of action with its unitary model. This model defines society as a system of action, assumes integration through stratification, and declares that shared values, shared ideas about means and ends, and a common sense of solidarity are necessary prerequisites for the existence of society. The model claims to be universal in its application to all societies (Smith, M. G. 1965a: vii-ix, 1965b: 1-4).

Consequently, Raymond T. Smith, one of the proponents of the unitary model, observes that in the West Indian colonial societies where groups of varying cultures were held together by the English Crown for a long period of time, a set of common values eventually emerged for the whole society. The general policies of the colonial administration, emphasizing Christianity, education, respect for law and order tended to create some degree of commitment to values that are shared by all of the constituting segments (Smith, R. T., 1966: 51). While elaborating upon his assessment of the shared values, Smith explained that his statement does not imply that West Indian societies are held together strongly by a sense of social solidarity, or to use Durkheim's expression, by a common conscience. According to Smith the integration level of the West Indian society may be perceived around the recognition and acceptance of the idea of the superiority of English culture. The element of normative consensus (Max Weber) among the various segments of the society is noted in their common attitude toward English culture. It is due to the acceptance of the superiority of the English culture (a common culture value) that "things in these societies tended to be judged in terms of a comparison with English culture and English standards, and that the whole structure of the society including the ranking system tended to acquire a 'legitimacy' in terms of these standards and values" (Smith, R. T. 1966: 51). Raymond Smith thus suggests that the West Indian society is not a plural society in terms of M. G. Smith's analysis. It has only two sets of stratification structures. One is based on social status, economic power and political authority without any reference to ethnic background of the individual. The other is a set of status and power relationships based on the division of the population by racial and ethnic background. Thus, according to Raymond Smith, conceptualization of the West Indian society without recognizing the relationship of ethnic group stratification to social class stratification would be weak and defenseless.

My discussion has, so far, centered around a survey of the research approaches to the study of Caribbean societies and has focused especially on a critical examination of the scope and the limitations of the two major competing models that have been used for the study of the multi-ethnic, multi-racial, and so-called complex societies of the area. Such discussions are extremely relevant and instructive because they illustrate the different types of questions that might be raised in a study of the East Indian group in Guyana. For example, it may be asked whether, in a unified political system such as is present in Guyana, the existence of different cultural patterns placed in a unique arrangement of contact situations would result in the modification of existing cultural patterns or would contribute to their persistence. It may further be investigated how differently the cultural patterns would respond to the economic and political changes within the territorial boundaries of a society. More importantly it may be examined whether the desire to achieve the intrinsic rewards which result from group cohesion contributes to the persistence of different cultural patterns, or whether a new idiom reflecting cultural unity based on some basic minimum shared values would eventually emerge at the total societal level. Conversely, in case the persistence of the cultural patterns has been maintained over a long period covering almost a century, it may be asked what factors, other than the external force of colonial administration, have contributed to the common participation of the cultural segments in the political and economic life of the colony. Related to this is an important question which asks, whether, in cases where segmentation of the society is found to run parallel to the ethnic-cum-racial affiliations of the people, separate cultural patterns exist at all generational levels of each segment, or whether the differences in cultures between the constituent segments are differential at different generational levels?

The answers to these enquiries, regardless of whether the Guyanese society as a whole or as a constituent segment thereof is to be studied, seem to lie in a combination of the two competing models. Since my research is confined to the East Indian group only, we would try to see how the two models, plural and consensual, could be combined to provide us with an understanding of the continuities and changes in the cultural pattern of the East Indian society in the Guyanese social context.

It has been illustrated elsewhere that the emerging Guyanese society can be understood only against the background of social historical events and trends. The beginning of the indenture system in Guyana, the economic and political motives behind the immigration of the indentured laborers in the colony, and the interplay of the social relationships between the newly arrived indentured laborers and the emancipated slave laborers account for the ethnic division of the Guyanese society. The Indian immigration was finally terminated in 1917. Consequently, we now find the members of from four to five generations of descendants of Indian immigrants living in the colony, the fifth generation being still in the stage of infancy.

For the purpose of our analysis, the people of the first and second generation may be grouped together forming one category in terms of the commonality of their attitudes, shared concerns and the identical nature of the problems that they faced in the process of adjustment with the local socio-economic environments. Similarly members of the third and fourth generation can be placed in another category on the basis of some of their outstanding shared characteristics. For the sake of convenience we will call the members of the first and second generations the "older generation", and the members of the third and fourth generations the "younger generation". The notable distinctions between the two categories are as follows.

The people of the first and second generations are mostly indentured laborers brought from India with their offspring being born in Guyana. They speak their native language. They remember the places of their origin in India. They trace their ancestry to three or four generations on the ascending scale. Most of the people of this category did not receive any formal education in Guyana. They did not avail themselves of western education because the educational institutions were run by Christian missionaries. Respect for the old traditions, the maintenance of orthodox religious practices, and the desire for the continuation of the old social order and other authentic forms of Indian life are the hallmarks of the older generation. These are their prime values.

In the course of time, due to a higher rate of fertility in this group, the people of the third and fourth generations came to constitute a sizable part of the total community. The changes in this category of the East Indian population were so pronounced that they formed a distinctive group within the larger group of the Indian society. This younger generation is characterized by distinctive traits. The third generation people can understand the Indian language but can not speak it at all. The fourth generation have lost even this characteristic. Comprehension of the native language became rare and exceptional. Only a few words pertaining to the basics of life such as food, clothing, and belief systems were left as part of their vocabulary. People in the younger generation can not name the places in India from which their ancestors came. They can trace their ancestry back only to their Guyanese ancestors. Their knowledge about Indian tradition is derived from secondary sources and represents, for the most part, a watered down version of the original tradition.

As observed by Kroeber, the "cultural phases associated with age may be assumed to correspond to changes taking place in the culture rather than to reflect chronic or static lines of segregation, like those between social classes" (Kroeber 1948: 274-75). Thus in order to understand the similarities in the cultural forms that run through all generations and also the differences in the attitudes of the members of the two different categories, it appears that the approaches of both the unitary and the reticulate models will have to be employed simultaneously to develop a total picture of the East Indian culture. The plural model explains adequately the existing institutional arrangements in a given segment of the society as compared to the other constituent groups of the societal whole. However, it needs to be emphasized that no segment of the society lives in complete isolation. A focus on the institutional arrangements of a society without recognizing the articulation of the institutions to meet the pressures of the economic and political forces operative both at the local and national levels is bound to inhibit an understanding of the dynamic dimension of the society. It will also fail to portray the emerging intersectional relationships between the different components of the society. An insight into the emerging cultural segment can be obtained through the use of the consensual model which, as was pointed out earlier, tends to emphasize the common consensus and the unifying factors in a society. Thus it is suggested that when the carriers of a culture are placed in a set of controlled social environments that inhibit contact from the parent culture, and when the situation generates constant interaction with other cultural segments of the larger society, the phenomena of cultural continuities and changes should not be determined by simply looking into the contents and forms of the culture, but by examining the meanings and functions that the same contents and forms may provide at different times to different categories of people within the cultural segment. In the given situation it is my hypothesis that, under the pressure of the vehement and persuasive forces of change, the cultural contents and forms may be retained to serve as symbols of ethnic identity, but the more important aspects of culture, that is, the intrinsic meanings and functions of the forms, change selectively to permit adjustment of the culture to the emerging patterns of the larger society.

CHAPTER THREE

# The Development of a Multi - Racial Society

IT MAY SEEM on the surface a rather elusive parallelism, but, if oil may be called the "Black Gold" of the Middle East for its function and role of economic transformation of the local society from a general level of poverty to a state of selective affluence, by the same token, sugar may be termed the "White Gold" of Guyana. Sir Walter Raleigh's restless search for El Dorado, the fabulous and mythical city of gold that led him to the coast of Guyana seems, in this context, an interesting coincidence. The "Oil Kings" of the Middle East have much in common with the "Sugar Kings" of British Guyana in their exploits except, perhaps, for one basic difference; in the process of achieving their ends, the former required a more advanced technology and "well greased" machinery and less human labor to operate its movement, whereas the latter needed more manpower and an organized labor force to grease the machinery itself.

By the time the splintered territorial occupations of the English were integrated into the geographically contiguous unit of Guyana, and were administered through a centralized government located in Georgetown (1831), the basic texture of its economy was more or less well laid out. The Spaniards were the first Europeans to arrive in Guyana and the Dutch were the first to open it to colonization (1580). The Dutch traders, "Patroons"[1] as they were called, had been allowed by their chartered company[2] during its first phase of 24 years to establish settlements and trading posts in Essequibo, Berbice, and Pameroon. They were primarily involved in exchanging their own trade items for cotton, dyes and lumber obtained from the local Indian sources. Their agricultural activity was confined to the cultivation of tobacco, coffee and cocoa along the banks of the rivers. Occasional and sporadic attempts at cane cultivation by the Dutch "Patroons"[3] yielded encouraging results but the

---

1 "Patroons" were the traders who were given feudal rights if they were able to buy river basin lands and settle 50 people on them.
2 The first chartered West Indies Company of the Netherlands was incorporated in 1621 for a period of 24 years. The Charter being renewed in 1647 for another 25 years (Smith, R. T. 1962: 14).
3 Many accounts testify that Abraham Van Peere was perhaps the first patroon who started a sugar plantation at Berbice in 1637. His example was subsequently followed by many patroons in other parts of the colony.

British rivalry[4] made Dutch prosperity only a shortlived phase. The next twenty-five years witnessed a shift from a predominantly trading economy to the more profitable business of the sugar plantation. The shift was activated by two preeminent factors. First, to regulate their trades the Dutch West Indies Company acquired the services of Laurens Storm van's Gravesande as secretary and bookkeeper in 1737, and later promoted him to "commandeur" in 1742. For his foresight, administrative skill, and devotion he deserves a place among the greatest men in the history of Guyana. Despite every possible opposition from the Board of Directors, who were highly conscious of their superior positions, Gravesande succeeded in opening the coastlands of Guyana to settlers of all nations giving them immunity from taxation for ten years (1746). This step by Gravesande paved the way for the second factor. The rich coastlands of Guyana, most favorable for sugar cultivation, lured British planters from Barbados and other Caribbean Islands where, because of soil depletion, the plantations were already showing signs of diminishing returns. With the active participation of the English who "spared neither trouble, industry, nor cost" (Gravesande), the number of sugar plantations grew rapidly. By 1760 the British were more numerous than the Dutch in the colony. It is difficult to determine the actual number of sugar plantations that were then in operation. The inaccuracy of the records reflect the nature of the sugar operation. It was not unusual for the planters to turn in false statements to avoid payment of taxes. The registers maintained by the Dutch Company do not show any consistency in the number of plantations or in the number of laborers employed in each county. The estates of the Berbice Association, a separate undertaking which was independent of the Dutch Company, were managed by Master Planters and no record exists of their number. Over and above the Association's estates there were a number of private plantations owned by independent settlers, who were least interested in placing their possessions on record. After scanning all the available contemporary sources Raymond T. Smith could make only an apologetic effort to record 411 plantations by the end of 1769.[5]

*Table 1*
*Plantations in Guyana by 1769*

| County | No. of Plantations | Year |
|---|---|---|
| Berbice & Canje | 93 + 20 = 113 | 1762 |
| Demarara | 206 | 1769 |
| Essequibo | 92 | 1769 |
| Berbice Association Estates | (not known) | |
| Total | 411 | |

4 Lord Willoughby wiped out flourishing Dutch settlements by the use of his forces from Barbados in 1665.
5 This table has been prepared from Raymond Smith's discussion of the subject in his publication: *British Guiana* (Smith, R. T. 1962: 16-17). For the collection of his material on this period he has leaned heavily on two volumes of excerpts from Gravesande's official dispatches published by the Hakluyt Society (English translation C. A. Harris & J. A. J. de Villiers (ed.) *Storm Van's Gravesande: The Rise of British Guiana* (1911).

The figures given above are admittedly far from satisfactory in terms of presenting the exact picture, yet they are sufficient in that they are symptomatic of a significant shift in Guyana's economic structure from primitive and small scale cultivation to an "agri-industrial" economy based on sugar plantations.

It is in the nature of Guyanese coastal sugar plantations to succeed only if operated on a large scale and supported by an elaborate system of canals and dykes for the controlled inflow and outflow of the water. Individual planters with fragmented holdings on coastland situated below sea level were confronted with problems of Atlantic tides on one side and mangrove swamps on the other. These problems could not possibly be resolved by piecemeal efforts. A transition in sugar production from "engenho" (small family owned mill) to "usina" (big manufacturing establishment, great mechanized factory) was inescapable. A "Plantocracy" consisting of a few wealthy planters having vast acreage under cultivation which yielded, in return, a high profits which could be reinvested in the long range development of land, became an economic necessity. Obviously an agri-industrial complex of such dimensions had to be dependent upon the supply of a large tractable labor force, and this necessitated the import of a sizable number of slaves from the neighboring islands in the Caribbean and from Africa. In fact, Dalton observes, "the value of an estate was largely the value of the slaves upon it; so much so that this formed the most convenient criterion for taxation purposes" (1855: 396 Vol. I). It is not surprising therefore that the growth and development of the sugar plantation paralleled the course of development of slavery in Guyana. Slaves were imported in large numbers, as were horses, for the use of planters to man the slaves. It was noted often that it was more important for the Captain of a ship to account for the death of a horse than for the death of a slave (Swan 1957: 38). Dutch colonial laws were permissive in allowing atrocities on slaves. "Dutch law permitted punishments as atrocious as the crimes themselves. The treatment of the slaves by the planters was in general, cruel and in places sadistic" (Swan 1957: 38). This then was the local scene.

## The British Occupation

As a part of the prelude to the drama of the power struggle[6] in Europe, Britain entrenched herself well in the colony and by 1803 she replaced Dutch control and took over the complete administration of Guyana. In 1831 all three colonies, Essequibo, Demarara and Berbice were united under one administra-

---

6   In 1792 Holland became involved in the wars of the French Revolution. The Prince of Orange escaped to England to protect himself against the forces of Revolution which established the Batavian Republic in the Netherlands. British forces in Barbados availed of the opportunity to capture the Dutch Colony in 1796. At the Peace of Amiens in 1802 the captured Colony was restored to Holland. A year later, however, war broke out again. This time the English sent an expeditionary force under Hood and annexed the colony for the crown.

tion with headquarters in Georgetown, and this area was named British Guiana. These events marked the beginning of the phase of Guyanese history with which we are primarily concerned.

The British occupation of Guyana was followed by the passage of legislation by the home government which favored the English planters and helped to protect their sugar interests. The satisfaction of the planters was, however, not unmixed with anxieties. The anti-slavery group in England, led by Thomas Fowell Buxton, William Wilberforce, Lord Brougham and others had by this time gained substantial support in the British Parliament, so much so that Fox introduced the Anti-Slavery Bill which eventually brought an end to the slave trade in 1808. A full account of the Abolition Movement in the Western world, encompassing all its complexities, would be out of place here. Nevertheless it is relevant, in passing, to note that the closing decades of the Eighteenth Century evinced a striking social phenomenon—the growth of altruism—as the upper and middle classes began to think seriously about the lot of the people placed in the lower stations of life. The new humanitarianism severely criticized such inhuman practices as child and female labor, long factory hours, atrocities in prison, and lack of education facilities at home, and pitted itself against traffic in human beings abroad. "The Slave trade and African bondage" remarks Ragatz, "were anachronism in a world, animated by the new spirit of egalitarianism and brotherhood" (1963: 239). Tensions in master-slave relationships had been manifested as early as 1763 in "slave insurrection" in Berbice County. Conditions had not since improved.[7] The working conditions of the slaves had caused such an ugly and inhuman social scene that in spite of planters' delegations, petitions to His Majesty's Government, and even the extensive use of pressure groups, the Anti-Slavery Movement gained an edge over the protectors of the plantation interests.[8] In England the image of the planter was often that of a vile, social criminal.

> Old ladies (both male [?] and female) and Sunday School children were taught that the West Indian Planter was the vilest and most diabolical personage on the face of the globe. If one of them resided in the neighborhood he was pointed out as an ogre who fattened on the blood of the poor negro. He had none of the natural feelings of mankind—not an atom of pity or a grain of feeling—but delighted in tormenting and grinding his slaves underfoot. (Rodway 1891: 2)

The slave insurrection of 1823 and the execution of the London Missionary Society's John Smith, popularly known in Guyana as "Martyr Smith", added fuel to the fire. The Act of Abolition was finally passed and became law on

---

7  The total number of slaves imported could not be ascertained from the records, but at the time of first registration in 1817 their number was recorded as 101,712. Just 17 years later in 1834 when the slaves were freed and compensation was awarded their number had dwindled to 84,915. This high percentage of deaths among slaves can be explained only in terms of the subhuman living and working conditions on the plantations, and the acute malarial climate which took its own share in the loss of life.

8  For activities of the Society of West Indian Planters and Merchants which combated the abolition movement both in and out of the parliament see Ragatz 1963: 267-72.

August 1, 1834. According to this Act the termination of slavery on August 1, was to be followed by a six year period of apprenticeship during which the slaves were to be required to work as apprentices with reduced hours of daily labor. Even this provision had to be terminated on July 12, 1848, before its stipulated time.

This brief resumé of historical events has been presented here with the hope of explaining some of the socio-economic changes that occurred in Guyana during the period that followed the Act of Abolition. The Act may be characterized as a turning point in the history of Guyana in the sense that the age-old "Master-Slave" relationship on the plantations was changed henceforward into a new model of "Landlord-Tenant" relationship. Thus, abolition suddenly unleashed forces of change and set in motion developments which led to the emergence of patterns of culture and racial pluralism which to a great extent persist even today.

To most of the ill-informed slaves, emancipation meant cessation from labor, the end of treadmilling, flogging and the cat, the termination of iron chains and stocks, and the beginning of freedom to do as they pleased without accompanying responsibility. Many of them believed that they would now be able to live like their "Massa" (Master). Given the conditions under which they had existed, it is no wonder that the slaves-turned-laborers felt no commitments to their jobs. They took holidays for weeks and even months, and eventually only half of the males and a tenth of the females resumed work for hire (Rodway 1891: 30). After collecting their compensation documents or cash of £50/12/1 per head, many of them walked away from the plantations to Georgetown in search of lighter jobs.[9] No amount of pressure, neither the allurement of reduced hours of work, nor the bait of higher wages, induced them to return to their jobs regularly. The harsh memories of the days of slavery and the way in which they had been ruthlessly suppressed for any uprising, left little incentive for the freemen to again work on plantations. Good will between planters and the Negro was completely destroyed. Thus many of the laborers chose to establish independent villages. They grouped themselves into large bands, bought estates collectively, and started cooperative villages by dividing the land among themselves. More often than not they would organize themselves into work gangs headed by leaders who negotiated on their behalf with the planters for jobs on contract basis. Their first preference was, however, to work on their own lands. Plantation work was a secondary choice and was generally done only when more money was needed to supplement the income from their own farms. A normal pattern developed in that after finishing their contract, they would move to other places like migratory laborers. Most of them were ambitious to acquire, if possible, blue or white collar jobs in the capital. This halfhearted commitment of labor created a crisis in the sugar industry. The

---

9 At this point there were 84,915 slaves in the colony. The slave compensation provided under the Act, an amount of £ 4,297,117/10/6 which was distributed £ 50/12/1 per person (Rodway 1891: 24).

production of sugar fell sharply by almost 40 per cent (Weber 1931: 196). The average cost of production of a hogshead of sugar in Guyana was $98.81, while the ruling price in the world market was only $86.40 (Skinner 1955: 35). To face the competition, planters resorted to the reduction of wages. Under old conditions the reduction of wages would have been accepted with a minimum of resistance, but in the face of changed social conditions, the laborers resisted, resulting in wildcat strikes and labor riots, dislocation in the chain of labor activities, failure of the sugar crop, and eventually a decrease in the value of the plantation. It was for these reasons that the eminent author of Guyanese history, James Rodway, characterizes this phase of history as the "Period of Ruin" (Rodway 1891). However, Governor Barkley, a typical colonial administrator, reacted to the situation in a different way. According to him, freeholding by the freeman was a "crying evil." The men who preferred to work on their own lands rather than on the staple, sugar, were "guilty of an offense against patriotism, if not against the morals" (Skinner 1955).

The outlook for the planters was now very dismal. It naturally followed that some of them began to look to other countries with a view toward importing immigrants to meet the labor shortage. The result of their efforts was the introduction of new elements into the socio-cultural matrix of the Guyanese population.

Importation of wage laborers as a substitute for slave labor was not a new idea. It had been contemplated as early as 1811 to have emigrants brought from China, but the planters were mentally unprepared at that time to bargain away their coveted position of master-patron for that of the landlord-tenant type of relationship. The idea was, therefore, not translated into action. Under the pressure of the new situation, they realized that a large scale immigration was the only answer to the problem of salvaging their industry. Attempts were made to import Portuguese immigrants from Madeira and to encourage migration from the West Indian Islands. These attempts were met with little measurable success due to skepticism on the part of prospective emigrants as to their future status in the colony and the opposition of their respective local governments (Jagan 1967: 38). Meanwhile some French experiments with Indian emigrants in Bourbon (1830) had established the fact that "Indians made excellent labourers". This observation directed the attention of Guyanese planters toward India. With the initiative of John Gladstone, father of the famous British Liberal statesman and holder of two plantations in Guyana, permission was obtained from the Government of India to import immigrants from India provided they were indentured for a specified term of 5 years, and that certain specific facilities were assured in return for their services.[10] A return passage to India after the expiration of the contract period, in case laborers were unwilling to renew their contract, was included as one of the terms of the contract. Once the details were worked out, the first group of Indian "indentured laborers," 396 in number, were brought in 1838 on two ships,

---

10  For details on terms and conditions of work for Indian indentured labor see Nath 1950: 13.

the Whitby and the Hesperus. "Thus commenced the coolie immigration which was destined to revolutionize the whole colony and become a most important factor in its progress" (Rodway 1891: 93). The Indian laborers were popularly called "coolies" (a term still used in India for porters and hired laborers) or "East Indians," in order to distinguish them from the American Indians, generally called Amerindians, who were the original inhabitants of the colony. The first experiment with East Indian labor did not prove a success. At the end of a five year contract in 1843, only 60 out of 396 laborers agreed to stay in the colony, 2 absconded from plantations and 98 died. The remaining 236 preferred to return home (Nath 1950: 21). The phenomenal death toll of almost 24.7 per cent and the mass return of approximately 60 per cent illustrate the dissatisfaction of the Indian laborers. A general state of frustration and disillusionment among the indentured laborers arose partly from the gross ill-treatment of the immigrants by the plantation managements, and partly from the ignorance of those in position of authority and their inability to understand and appreciate the Indian customs, traditional ways, food habits and caste-based social structure. This lack of understanding is illustrated by a quotation from W. B. Wolesely, a member of a three man commission appointed to inquire into the problems of East Indians. He noted:

> Unfortunately the bright beams of Christianity have not shown among them and it is much to be lamented that they are left so entirely destitute of religious instructions as scarcely to be raised above the beasts of the field (Nath 1950: 18).

A lack of understanding of the caste restriction is reflected in a report by Dr. E. M. L. Smith, Surgeon General of the Government Hospital who remarked:

> When coolies were admitted to the hospital they not only brought their cooking vessels, but they were accompanied by three of their own cooks, as they positively refused to taste any food not prepared in their own vessels and by one of their number. They likewise rejected any but the peculiar food sanctioned by their religious tenets (Nath 1950: 18).

Reports on the Indian miseries echoed in the British Parliament as well as in the chambers of Indian Government. The Colonial Gazette (London) reported that "slavery under another name had been sanctioned in Mauritius and Demarara. The coolies were also like the slave apprentices." In his minutes dated July 3, 1838, Lord Auckland, then Governor General of India, strongly recommended appointment of a committee to investigate the matter before the policy of emigration continued to further feed British Colonies. Consequently, an embargo was imposed on emigration from India from July 11, 1838 pending receipt of the report from an enquiry committee appointed for the purpose.

The planters were once again left in despair. They now had to resort to other possible sources of labor. Various countries and areas such as England, Ireland, Germany, Southern Europe, Malta, Madeira, Egypt, Brazil and islands of the West Indies were explored to fill the labor gap caused by the withdrawal of Negro laborers and the suspension of the supply from India, but all sources proved unsatisfactory because, in most cases, the laborers were either unable to withstand the blasting heat of the tropical sun or had little requisite skill for agricultural work on the plantation.

The Portuguese, who had proved successful to some degree in the past (1834), were given another try in 1841. They came exclusively from Madeira Island which had been affected with widespread famines during the 1840's and 50's. Initially 4729 Madeirans were imported. The temptation of higher wages attracted more laborers, this time generally those who had been engaged in agriculture. Fear of a labor drain alarmed the Madeiran Government which in turn imposed difficult passport requirements and, thereby, restricted the flow of the Portuguese source. Labor managed to come, nevertheless. Their secret migration has been recorded by Dalton (1855: 462), and Harcourt (1853: 55). In total, 30,126 Portuguese had arrived in the colony by 1882, but prospects for future import became dim because of local Madeiran opposition and restriction. At first the Portuguese worked on plantations but gradually they moved away from the fields into the towns where they established themselves in commercial enterprises. Hickerson has attributed this shift from plantations to business as the main cause of a high mortality rate among Portuguese (1954). This would not appear to be true, since the mortality rate of the East Indians was by far the highest of all other ethnic groups involved, and yet they did not move into urban areas in search of their survival. Eventually very few Portuguese were left on plantations, and, thus, they came to be identified as independent, urbanized businessmen.

Another source of labor supply was opened in 1841 with immigrants from Sierra Leone, Africa. In terms of an ordinance full payment was provided for expenses involved in conducting immigration. In addition, private enterprises were also granted bounties on the number of laborers they could manage to attract. All told, 13,264 laborers were imported from Sierra Leone by 1865. Hard work, severity of punishment, and the adverse accounts given by those who returned home after their contract period drained this source of supply as well. No more laborers arrived from Africa after 1865. This group eventually merged with the larger group of former African slaves, since their somewhat similar physical traits and cultural background afforded common bonds between them.

A Chinese source was tapped in 1853, one which had already been catering to the needs of other areas, such as Cuba. Most of the Chinese came from the southernmost coastal provinces of Fukien and Kuantang (Clementi 1915: 43). Once opened this source continued to provide sizable numbers of laborers until 1866. Their total number had by then reached 12,631. Henceforth, their immigration was reduced to a trickle, and only 903 were added to the previous number. By 1879 Chinese immigration stopped completely. Running into the heels of the Portuguese, the Chinese also moved from plantation to town and became a predominantly self-sustaining urban community. The reasons for their movement away from plantations were, however, entirely different. The Chinese had fewer females than any other ethnic group. The maximum ratio of Chinese females to males never rose above fourteen females to every hundred males (Clementi 1937: 272). The isolated area of Hopetown, where the Chinese were first placed in order to discourage their emigration away from the colony, did not provide enough gratification for their sexual needs. Inevitably the Hopetown scheme proved a failure. Not long after, most of the Chinese moved to cities where they invested their family savings in small commercial enterprises such as grocery stores, restaurants, and other similar business. At present, out of the total population of 4,074 Chinese in Guyana, 72.1 per cent are living in the cities of Georgetown, Amsterdam, and their suburbs.

In the meantime the islands of the West Indies contributed a substantial number of laborers. They provided 40,833 persons from 1835-1917. Most of these people, like the African laborers, eventually merged into the local Negro population.

A note is perhaps necessary, at this point, to explain the ever increasing need of the sugar industry in Guyana. The end of the slave trade (1808), the Abolition of Slavery (1834), and the termination of apprenticeship (1838), were the outstanding humane measures taken by the British Parliament for its colonies in West Indies. Much as they were aimed at strengthening the human cause in general, they threatened to become a major disaster to the sugar industry in the British colonies. As was stated earlier, the good will between the laborers and planters of Guyana had been damaged beyond repair, and this was expressed in terms either of mass withdrawal of laborers or of demands for exorbitant wages which the industry could not afford to pay. The industry, already depleted of labor, suffered an additional blow in the form of the leveling of the differential duty on sugar in the United Kingdom market. The free trade movement in the United Kingdom, under the banner of the Anti-Corn Law League, opposed the preferential policy that had hitherto favored colonial sugar over foreign sugar. A heavy duty imposed on foreign sugar had afforded protection to the colonial sugar industry. This duty was equalized by 1854 through a series of measures. The foreign sugar imported from Cuba, Brazil, and other areas was grown by slave laborers whose ways and methods were well under the control of their master-producers. Once deprived of the protective duties, the colonial sugar industry was left with only one course of action: to import the largest number of laborers from all available sources and thus create internal competition among the laborers forcing them to accept jobs at reduced wages.

While attempts were being made to obtain indentured laborers from different available sources (some of which have been described above), certain political factors and natural adversities were working in India which developed into a major economic crisis. The impact of the crisis cannot be measured in statistical terms. It can be gauged only in terms of the historical fact and the social reality that a large segment of the Indian population (i.e., peasants), known to be traditionally shy in terms of spatial mobility, was pressured to major dispersal in search of survival. The factors were as follows:

1. Under constant pressure from the growing textile industry at home, the

British Parliament in 1720 imposed an absolute prohibition on the import or consumption of Indian calicoes and muslin. The back door smuggling of Indian muslin continued despite restrictive measures. On finding that Indian muslin was still posing a threat to the textile industry at home, British administrators chopped the fingers of known handloom workers in Bengal. The whole industry, which functioned on a cottage level in the villages, was thus destroyed, and the people were forced to live either by agriculture, or by producing raw materials needed for the manufacturing industry in Great Britain (Dutt 1916).

2. Even agriculture did not provide relief to the uprooted cottage industry craftsmen. After receiving the grant of Diwanee from the Nawab of Bengal in 1765, the British East India Company fixed the land tax in Bengal at over 90 per cent. Similarly, land taxes of 80 per cent were imposed in Northern India on the Ceded Districts and conquered areas of Uttar Pradesh lying between the Jamuna and the Ganges. The economic distress that resulted from these measures was such that it drew adverse criticism even from English historians.[11]

3. Over and above this, the major portion of Northern India was frequented by many famines during the 19th century (1804, 1837, 1861, 1877, 1889, 1889-1900).

All of these factors caused a major upheaval in the economic life of the people. Villages were deserted and a large number of people left their homes and hearths in search of jobs elsewhere.

It was during this period of economic distress that planters made representation to the Colonial Office, pointing out the critical position of the sugar industry in Guyana. They requested the removal of the ban on emigration from India. Lord Stanley, then Secretary of State for the Colonies, finally yielded and agreed to allow a limited emigration. The Government of India acted accordingly and in 1844 emigration was resumed. Four years later, recognizing the needs of the industry, the British Government made loans available to the West Indies Administration. This made the import of indentured laborers easier. A steady stream of Indian immigrants flowed into Guyana. This flow did not stop until 1917 when due to heavy criticism from Indian national leaders, including Mahatma Gandhi, the Government of Indian passed legislation abolishing the indenture system. Thus, in spite of an initial setback in 1838, Indian immigration, when resumed in 1845, surpassed all other sources of labor supply and had amassed in the Colony by 1917, when the system ended, a huge labor force of 256,564. An additional 607 persons came later on private arrangements. Of the 256,564 laborers who came during the period 1845-1917, only 18,222 returned to India. These were accompanied by 5,123 who had been born in Guyana. Census reports and other population sources indicate that the total Indian population in 1917 was only 138,400.[12]

---

11  Colonel Brigs wrote in 1830 "a land Tax like that which now exists in India professing to absorb the whole of landlord's rent, was never known under any Government in Europe or Asia". Quoted by Romesh Dutt (1916)
12  Records of the Department of Education, Health, and Lands of the Government of India

Making allowance for the number of persons who may have died of natural causes, a loss in population of 99,442 (which may have been replenished, to some extent, by the persons born during this period), leaves a large gap that poses a pertinent problem for further investigation and research. Two major reasons for this population loss would be the miserable working conditions under the indenture system and the cultural choice of the East Indians to remain in the villages where health and safety measures remained by far the poorest in the whole colony. Of all the ethnic groups who came under the indenture system, the East Indians are the only group who stayed behind on the plantations or established their own rice farm villages. Though some of their descendants have recently moved to the towns to become lawyers, doctors, teachers, or businessmen, most of the East Indians have remained in the rural areas living in villages and working in the sugar cane or rice fields. For a long time malaria was the main health hazard and which took the heaviest toll of life. Since it has been conquered the Guyanese of East Indian descent have grown in number so fast that they now form the largest ethnic group in Guyana.

## Summary

Spaniards were first among European peoples to discover Guyana and the Dutch were the first to open it to colonization (1580). The unbroken account of Guyanese history, however, begins with the occupation of the colony by the English in 1831. During the British rule the three countries which now comprise the Colony (i.e. Demarara, Essequibo, and Berbice) were brought under a centralized administration and Guyana became one geographically contiguous political unit. In fine, a new colony was born.

The economy of the colony began with a simple barter system. Manufactured articles from Europe were exchanged for locally available raw materials such as annatto, balsam, cocoa, cotton, dyes, and lumber. By the middle of the eighteenth century, however, a shift was noted from pure trade activity in the river basins to cane cultivation in the fertile coastal strips. Situated below sea level, the coastal zone required a complex supporting system of drainage and irrigation if it was to be used for agricultural purposes. Such a system was expensive to construct and also involved problems that required highly specialized engineering skill for their solution. Sugar planters were the only ones who had resources equal to the problem. With a huge capital investment they cleared the forests, reclaimed the mangrove swamps, constructed canals and dykes and put the entire scheme of sugar plantations into operation. A large tractable labor force of slaves was brought from Africa to work on the canefields. After acquiring a more or less monopolistic control over the men and resources of the colony the sugar industry became the bulwark of the Guyanese economy. Sugar "reigned supreme."

The English, as stated above, had assumed complete political control of Guyana by 1831 but control by the Crown remained subject to the manipulative influence of the sugar industry. As a result, during the entire period of colonial rule Guyana was governed and administered with due reference to the financial interest of its sugar industry. The problems of the sugar industry, price fluctuations in the world sugar market, and labor shortage and supply acted selectively in shaping the policies of the colonial administration. It is no wonder that British Guiana is often nicknamed "Booker's Guiana" (Booker Brothers of England own all the sugar factories in Guyana and some of the biggest commercial enterprises in Georgetown).

More important perhaps than any other consequence of the sugar industry's presence in Guyana was the growth of a plural society comprising many ethnic groups and varying cultural systems. The need for controlled labor for the large scale cultivation of sugar cane led first to the introduction of slave labor from Africa, and when slavery was abolished, it paved the way for the immigration of indentured laborers from India, China, Madeira (Portuguese) and other sources. The exigencies of the sugar industry thus prepared a groundwork for the growth and emergence of the present day multi-racial and multi-cultural pattern of Guyanese society.

CHAPTER FOUR

# Land, Peoples, and Cultures of Guyana

"GUIANA" is a word of Amerindian origin which means "land of water." It is used to designate the region lying east of Venezuela and north of Brazil on the northeastern shoulder of the South American continent; an area of great rivers which receives a heavy annual rainfall. The area historically has been divided into three political units: French Guiana, Dutch Guiana (Surinam) and British Guiana. As compared to other British colonies in the West Indies, Guyana is by far the largest. Lying between 1° and 9° of northerly latitude and between 57° and 61° of westerly longitude it covers a land area of 83,000 square miles, almost equal to the size of Great Britain, or to the state of Idaho in the United States.

## Geographical Divisions

For the purpose of the present study Guyana can be divided into four different zones, situated one behind the other, parallel to the coastline. Bordering on the sea is the coastal zone (or Sugar Zone), a narrow strip of land about 15 to 20 miles in width and 270 miles in length. An overwhelming majority of the population lives in this area, and economically it is the most important part of Guyana, as all of the sugar estates and most of the rice fields, towns and villages are located in this region.

Flanked by the Atlantic Ocean on the north and the swampy backland waters on the south, this coastal zone, lying below sea level, is exposed on both sides to the constant threat of floods. The mean annual rainfall in this zone ranges from 80 inches in the East to 110 inches in the West. This heavy rainfall poses the threat of flooding. Artificial drainage and flood control are therefore major concerns of the local communities, sugar estates and the national government. A continuous belt of sea wall has been constructed facing the Atlantic to stop the inflow of water at high tides. The sea wall is further equipped with sluices (*khokas*) through which the outflow of the water is regulated. The swamp water on the opposite end is controlled by a "back dam." Water is discharged through sluices into a network of canals and trenches dug for the purpose of irrigation and drainage. The canals run on two different levels. Those of the higher level serve for irrigation and transport and those at the lower serve for drainage. This artificial system of irrigation and drainage plays a vital role in the existence of the people living in the coastal zone. Due to heavy silt formation regular upkeep and maintenance of the system is necessary.

Whereas general supervision and maintenance is taken care of by the Public Works Department, the local communities are responsible for seeing that the *khokas* are kept in good repair and that the trenches remain free of excess plant growth.

Lying behind the Coastal Zone is the Timber Zone, the only area from which timber has as yet been remuneratively brought to market. This area extends toward the interior as far as the lowest cataracts of the various rivers. It is at present impossible to cut timber profitably beyond these cataracts. Thus an imaginary line, roughly parallel to the sea coast and crossing each of the great rivers at the lowest cataract, can be drawn to define the Timber Zone. This area is very sparsely populated. Most of the economic activity is confined to logging, and many of the woodcutters work at this job for extra income during the idle periods in rice cultivation and sugar production.

The Timber Zone is immediately followed by the Forest Zone which includes almost three quarters of the whole colony. It is full of dense forests as yet fairly free of loggers and consists largely of valuable trees such as Greenheart, Mora, Crabwood and Wallaba. Of all these types of timber, Greenheart is the most valuable. It is a very hard wood and is used all over the world to build wharves and docks because it does not rot in the salt water of the sea. Except for the loggers, who are periodic visitors, the settled population of this area consists mainly of Amerindians living in several scattered villages.

The last of the three zones is the Interior Savannah which is situated farthest from the sea; it borders on Brazil from which it is separated by the Ireng and Takatu rivers. This area is generally called Rupununi after the main river of the Southwest of Guyana. The Interior Savannah Zone must be distinguished from the swampy areas immediately behind the coastal zone which are also called savanah. Like the Forest Zone this area is also very sparsely populated. Most of the inhabitants are Amerindians living in their own scattered village-like settlements.

**Climate**

Climate is an important factor in the daily life of every person in Guyana. It influences the food habits, dress patterns, house style, rhythm of life cycle, economic activities and the annual cycle of social events, such as marriages, religious ceremonies, rituals and festivals. Since 90 per cent of the total population live within the narrow strip of the "coastal zone" it is relevant in the context of this study to discuss only the climate of this area. Differences in other geographical divisions do exist, but have no major bearing on the life of the coastal people.

The Coastal Zone of Guyana is a part of the tropical world. Because it lies close to the equator, the sun strikes hot on the ground all year long. The mean temperature averages around 80° F with the daily range rarely exceeding 14° F. Days are hot but the nights are pleasant. The tropical heat during the daytime is somewhat neutralized by the constant breeze from the Atlantic (North East Trade Wind), but the humidity remains high at all times (average 80 per cent). Rainfall is high, averaging around 90 inches per annum, with a fluctuating range between 60 and 120 inches. Rain comes mainly during certain seasons as illustrated below in Table 2.

*Table 2*
*Annual Rainfall Distribution*

| Period | Rainfall Conditions |
|---|---|
| Mid-April-mid-August | Heavy rainfall |
| Mid-August-mid-November | Dry season |
| Mid-November-mid-February | Scattered rainfall |
| Mid-February-mid-April | Dry season |

## Population

Guyana is one of the few areas in the world which belies Malthusian proposition in the nature of its population problem. With 91.5 per cent of the people living on the narrow coastland it presents a somewhat deceptive picture of over-population and as such poses problems of high population pressures similar to those of any other tropical country. A high population pressure is often expressed as a matter of concern by the government officials. But when the pressure of numbers is calculated with reference to the country's total area, it is found that in terms of this ratio the country is very sparsely populated. With about 7.6 persons to the square mile, Guyana actually stands in need of a policy of population expansion. Guyana's population problem is therefore unique and interesting. The country is exposed simultaneously to the economic consequences of both overpopulation and that of underpopulation.

More interesting than this contrasting feature perhaps, are the nature and the racial components of the population. With the exception of 29,430 Amerindians (forming 4.6 per cent of the population) who live in the interior savannah, the entire population is comprised of the offspring of immigrants who were either brought forcibly as slaves or who volunteered to work as indentured laborers on sugar plantations during the 19th and early 20th centuries. As previously mentioned the slaves were all of African origin. The indentured laborers came from Africa as well as from various other areas such as China, Madeira (Portuguese) and India. Whereas Africans seem to have lost much of their native culture during the course of their settlement in Guyana, the indentured laborers retained the outstanding traits of their own respective cultures. Bound together by economic and political organizations, the assemblage of all within the small geographical unit of Guyana has created what one may call a "cultural galaxy"; a phenomenon which has provided a basis both for plural and consensual models of sociological analysis. The racial composition of the population, as revealed by the latest available population and vital statistics (December, 1964 estimates) is shown in the following table:

Table 3
Racial Composition of the Population (December 1964)

| Racial Group | Population | Percentage |
|---|---|---|
| East Indians | 320,070 | 50.2 |
| Africans | 199,830 | 31.3 |
| Mixed | 75,990 | 12.0 |
| Amerindians | 29,430 | 4.6 |
| Portuguese | 6,380 | 1.0 |
| Chinese | 3,910 | 0.6 |
| Europeans | 2,420 | 0.3 |
| Total | 638,030 | 100.0 |

In the past many more racial categories were recognized by the census authorities, but recently the scheme of racial classification has tended to correspond to the popular image of Guyana as "the land of Six Peoples." The population is divided into seven components, six of which are racial groups. The remaining category of "Mixed" represents those who are the results of miscegenation between the six groups, but especially between Negroes and Whites.

There is a tendency in Guyana to treat Amerindians as the original inhabitants, which they are; Africans as semi-original inhabitants or "creoles"; and all the other indentured laborers and their offspring as immigrants (M. G. Smith, 1965a: 13). Even though such a classification may not be truly justified because many of the Africans came to Guyana as indentured laborers, the self-perceived images of the groups, by which they classify themselves as non-immigrants and immigrants, provide a sociological basis for the study of group dynamics. Treated as such Table 3 shows not only the numerical strength of each group but also demonstrates that the "immigrants" form 52.1 per cent of the Guyanese population today (Mixed group excluded). The scale of immigration during the period of indenture (1835-1917) was obviously very high in that the population balance has tilted in favor of immigrants within the fifty years following this period. The Registrar General's estimates and the reports of the Immigration Agent-General show that, at times (1841 and 1874), the rate of immigration reached as high as 430 and 400 per thousand respectively, and the population of the country rose from 98,000 in 1831 to 296,041 in 1911. The Immigration Reports further explain that the immigrants from each area came in groups and that subsequent to their settlement they worked and lived in such close geographical proximity that the in-group interaction was more spontaneous than planned. Under the circumstances it is imperative for any social scientific study that its problems should be phrased in terms of groups, group relations and structures rather than in terms of the assimilation of individuals.

Among the immigrants, East Indians form by far the largest single group of the population. They account for 50.2 per cent of the total population, which is more than the combined total of all other racial groups. The bulk of the East

Indians live in the countryside. They work on the sugar plantations or own rice fields. In 1911, 94 per cent of the East Indians lived in rural areas and accounted for 81.6 per cent of the farmers and agricultural laborers in Guyana. No major changes were to be noted in this figure prior to 1931, a year in which 71.5 per cent of the country's agricultural labor force was still comprised of East Indians (Nath 1950: 216). In the 1930's and 1940's, however, some changes could be noted. The East Indian literacy rate in English, the official language of the country, increased to 30 per cent, and there was also a corresponding increase of East Indians in non-agricultural employment. The major occupational trend, nevertheless, remains unchanged. East Indians still dominate the rural scene and continue to fill a higher percentage of agricultural occupations. Of the total number of East Indians, 86.7 per cent live in rural areas and they form only 22 per cent of the urban population of the country.

The second largest group is that of the Negroes, who form 31.3 per cent of the total population. From the very beginning, this group has been widely exposed to miscegenation with other racial groups. During the period of slavery, it was not uncommon that Negro females were used as concubines by the white members of the plantation management (Roberts 1948: 188). Later, in the 1830's when immigration was opened and male laborers of different races were brought into the country accompanied by a very low percentage of females, the intermingling of Negro females and immigrant males became fairly common. Conditions became even more conducive to racial intermingling after 1950 when a high mortality rate among Negro males brought about a preponderance of females over males in the native population (Roberts 1948: 188). These factors explain the high percentage of "Mixed" in the census reports. The census reports also establish that among the "Mixed" group there is an outstandingly common element of Negro genes mixed with the genes of other racial stocks.[1]

As stated previously the Negroes dispersed from the plantations at the end of slavery and migrated heavily toward the urban centers. Today they account for 49 per cent of the urban population (56.8 per cent of the Negroes live in the rural areas).

The other racial groups such as Portuguese, Chinese and Europeans constitute only 2.5 per cent of the total population. A steady decline in the strength of these groups between 1911-1960 is noticeable. They are largely concentrated in towns.

It is difficult to understand the demographic patterns and population trends without reliable and detailed quantitative data. Tables 4 and 5, prepared on the basis of information collected from different sources help to explain some of the more pronounced population trends and the relative positions of the different racial groups in the country.

Tables 4 and 5 show clearly that the population of Guyana has increased

---

1 According to the census of 1851 the sex ratios of the different racial groups were as follows: East Indians—233 females to 1000 males; Portuguese—639 females to 1000 males; Chinese—149 females to 1000 males (G. W. Roberts 1948: 186).

Table 4
Percentage Distribution of Racial Population 1911-1960

| Year | Total Population | Percentage Distribution | | | | | | | |
|---|---|---|---|---|---|---|---|---|---|
| | | East Indians | Negroes | Mixed | Portuguese | Europeans | Amerindians | Chinese | Other |
| 1911 | 296,041 | 42.7 | 39.0 | 10.2 | 3.4 | 1.3 | 2.3 | 1.0 | 0.1 |
| 1921 | 297,691 | 42.0 | 39.4 | 10.3 | 3.1 | 1.0 | 3.0 | 1.0 | 0.2 |
| 1931 | 310,933 | 42.0 | 39.9 | 10.9 | 2.8 | 0.7 | 2.7 | 0.9 | 0.1 |
| 1946 | 375,701 | 43.5 | 38.2 | 10.0 | 3.0 | | 4.3 | 0.9 | 0.1 |
| 1960 | 560,330 | 48.0 | 32.8 | 11.9 | 0.6 | | 4.5 | 0.7 | 1.5 |
| 1964 | 638,030 | 50.2 | 31.3 | 12.0 | 1.0 | 0.3 | 4.6 | 0.6 | ... |

Sources: a) G. W. Roberts, "Some Observations on the Population of British Guiana," *Population Studies*, II, No. 2 (1948).
b) Registrar General; Annual Reports.
c) Report of the British Guiana Commission of Inquiry (October, 1965).

Table 5
Inter-Censal Annual Rates of Increase, by Race, 1911-1960 (per cent per year)

| Period | East Indians | Negroes | Mixed | All other races excluding Amerindians | Total Colony excluding Amerindians |
|---|---|---|---|---|---|
| 1911-21 | —0.4 | +0.1 | +0.1 | —0.6 | +0.0 |
| 1921-31 | +0.4 | +0.6 | +1.0 | —1.3 | +0.5 |
| 1931-46 | +1.4 | +1.0 | +0.8 | +0.4 | +1.1 |
| 1946-60 | +3.6 | +1.9 | +4.2 | +0.5 | +2.9 |

Source: Peter Newman, *British Guiana: Problems of Cohesion in an Immigrant Society* (London: Oxford University Press, 1964).

substantially during the last fifty years. It has tripled since 1911 and each census report has recorded a steady upward trend in the rate of growth. An almost meteoric rise in population occurred in the years 1931-1946 when the number rose from 310,933 in 1931 to 375,701 in 1946. An equally significant rise was recorded during the subsequent period (1946-1960). This sudden increase can be primarily attributed to the complete eradication of malaria in the coastal zone through an effective DDT campaign from 1945-47. Whereas malaria eradication was no doubt a major single factor for lowering the death rate, other factors, such as the increase in per capita income during World War II and the increase in the natural population growth before this period, also account for the rise in the population figure (Newman 1964: 37-38). Table 5 shows an interesting feature of the demographic pattern. It establishes that the general population growth in Guyana was overwhelmingly influenced by the rapid growth of the East Indian segment. During the period 1946-60 the East Indian population of 0-4 age group increased by 100.7 per cent. There were notable increases in all other selected age groups but most noticeable was the fact that in every age group the rates of increase of the East Indian sector were considerably higher than the corresponding rates for all the other races put together. An increase of 44 per cent for the age group 15-64 during the same period (1964-60) is highly significant since these persons are directly responsible for the high reproductive rates among East Indians and, thus, for the country as a whole. Using the year 1946 as a base, a random estimate of the Natural Increase rate (i.e. births over deaths) for the next 13 years was made with the help of available records in the office of the Registrar General. It was noted that whenever the Natural Increase rate for the whole colony increased, the corresponding increase in rate for East Indians was almost twice as high, and whenever there was a drop in rate for the whole country, this drop was similarly influenced by a decrease in the rate of the East Indians. During the period 1946-59, for example, the increase rate for all races was 4.9 per cent while that for the East Indians was 7.9 per cent. Likewise, during the period 1945-1949 the drop in the increase rate for the whole colony was 3.2 per cent while that for East Indians was 5.2 per cent. It is evident from these direct variations in rate that the contribution from the East Indian component of the population is determining the natural increase of the entire population of Guyana to the extent of almost 50 per cent. In 1946, the East Indians accounted for 45.6 per cent of the total population. By 1960 they reached 48 per cent, and in 1964 they formed over half the population of the whole country. It is to this component of the population that this study is particularly addressed.

**Administrative Structure**

Administratively speaking, Guyana is divided into three counties: Demarara, Essequibo and Berbice. These counties are named after three large rivers which emerge from the mountains in the interior and flow northward to the coastal zone where they meet the Atlantic. Of the three counties Demarara is the smallest in area, but ranks highest in importance. Its importance stems from the fact that it is highly industrialized, most urbanized and has the highest concentration of population. Above all, it houses the seat of the central government in its city of Georgetown.

The basic structure of the country's system of government indicates British influence. The three main organs of government in Guyana—the executive, legislature, and judiciary—are responsible to each other. None of them is completely autonomous and independent. The governor, appointed by the British Crown, is the executive head of the state, however under the terms of the present constitution, his functions resemble those of the constitutional monarch of England. The executive authority is actually exercised by a cabinet of ministers appointed by the prime minister, a position always held by the leader of the majority party or the largest party in the assembly. The legislative powers are vested in a unicameral legislature or assembly whose members are elected on the basis of proportional representation. In actual practice the party system functions in such a way that the legislature generally has to seek guidance from the executive branch in matters of initiation of legislation and in the performance of its regular legislative functions. Thus in this sense the legislative and executive branches are not independent of each other. Judicial authority resides in the Supreme Court. It is the highest court and final appellate body in the country, however, its members are appointed on the recommendation of the cabinet. Moreover, while exercising its powers to interpret the constitution, the Supreme Court functions as an important source of law. Thus, in the central government of Guyana, the executive, legislature, and judiciary which appear to exist as separate units are functionally intertwined in such a manner that their separation and independent operation is, in practice, unfeasible.

Keeping in mind this guiding principle of outward separation and inward amalgamation of the functions of the three basic organs of government, which operates at all levels of government, one can devise an administrative classification for the country consisting of four typological units.

1. *Cities.* The cities of Georgetown and New Amsterdam are administered by municipal corporations. Georgetown has a city council with a Lord Mayor who is elected by the council members. The Municipal Corporation performs a wide range of duties; cultural, educational, social and recreational. With the financial backing of the Central Government the council takes care of the planning and development of the town. The only other city in the country, New Amsterdam, has a similar administration. Georgetown, however, enjoys a higher status as the national capital.

2. *Sugar Estates.* As the huge industrial corporations, who not only own their sugar processing plants but also the vast tracts of adjoining lands used for plantations and residential colonies for their laborers, the sugar estates have come to assume the position of separate administrative units. They provide the general amenities of life for their laborers in the interests of their respective establishments. Under recent political changes (more specifically during the representative governments of the 1950's and 1960's) the sugar estate managements have been stripped of much of their administrative authority and have been obliged to function only as industrial establishments. In face of the rising tide of the nationalist movement, the old "paternalism" of the plantation management, which had stretched itself beyond industrial involvements to include among its functions the "proper" regulation of the social, moral, and religious life of the people, has now receded into the background. Nevertheless, even though the *de jure* authorities of the plantation management have been written off, elements of the traditional relationship between labor and management still survive, and the *de facto* powers of management continue to be exercised through many invisible means such as preferences in seasonal employment, job promotions, credit facilities and favors in the allotment of better houses.

3. *Unorganized Areas.* Most of the rural areas and the population residing thereon are subject to local governments. But like small islands located in the middle of large waters, there exist some areas in the coastland which may be

labeled as unorganized areas. "Usually unorganized areas are stretches of unkempt country with many ownerships, indifferent drainage facilities, poor roads and only such social services as the central government provides directly" (Marshall 1955: 10). Having been owned individually and neglected consistently it is not unusual that these areas remain outside the main stream of the country's overall development. The awareness of this developmental lag sometimes prompts the people to organize themsleves as cooperative units, collect "rates" on a voluntary basis, and join in schemes of local improvement such as road construction, maintenance of drainage, care of pasture land, and many other services normally provided by a local government. The unorganized areas, however, remain for the most part neglected and undeveloped.

4. *Local Authorities*. The Local Authorities form the lowest tier of the administrative structure. These are a form of local governments set up on a village level and run on the principle of cooperation and self help. Each Local Authority is comprised of a council elected by the village dwellers with a chairman as its head. Their lowest position in the administrative hierarchy, however, should not be misconstrued as also being the weakest. In principle they are assigned considerable powers and "exist to provide areas with [all of the] things they need" (Marshall 1955: 19).

The Local Authorities are multipurpose bodies which provide a number of services for the rural communities. Formulated strictly on the basic concept of local self-government they are given autonomy in the handling of most community problems. They are free to make their own policies, take care of their finances, collect "rates" and charges, and look after the administration and the economic problems of the community on a cooperative basis, within the framework of standing orders approved by the Central Government. Thus, each Local Authority becomes an integrated unit of social relationship, in which each incident such as birth, death, marriage, local feud, opening of a shop, construction of a new house, harvest of anyone's field, and even the travel of local residents to points outside the village, becomes a matter of common interest or concern. In fine, the Local Authority, in most cases, forms a social nucleus in which the participating members establish most of their primary and secondary group relationships and satisfy their corresponding needs. Our present unit of study, the village of Crabwood Creek, forms a Local Authority. The village life, its institutional patterns and the socio-cultural matrix of the community are therefore to be studied within the framework of the above administrative structure.

CHAPTER FIVE

# The Village of Crabwood Creek

ONE HUNDRED AND TWENTY MILES east of Georgetown, the capital of Guyana, the quiet and majestic River Corentyne meets the Atlantic and divides the northeastern shoulder of the South American continent into two "Guianas." On the eastern shore of the river one can observe a continuous green belt formed by the overgrowth of thick vegetation, and punctuated only by the tiny islands[1] looming out in the middle of the river. This green line is Nickerie, a part of Dutch Guiana otherwise known as Surinam. On the western shore the view is different. Instead of a green belt of vegetation, it is marked with a continuous row of houses, two stellings projecting deep into the river, the long chimneys of the Skeldon Sugar Factory emitting smoke, and many large and small boats floating on the surface of the water, all indicating life and a humdrum of human activity on the shore. This is Corentyne, the eastern end of Berbice County, Guyana. The locale of this study, Crabwood Creek, is situated in this area at the point where the fifty mile long arterial public road east of New Amsterdam ends, running, as it appears, frustratingly into savannahs bordered by thick jungles.

Like other parts of the colony, the county of Berbice was also taken away from the Dutch by the English (Sept. 24, 1803). It was subsequently merged (1831) with Essequibo and Demarara counties to form an integral part of Guyana. When Berbice became a British occupied territory, delimitation of the boundaries with the adjoining Dutch colony became a political necessity. Consequently an agreement was reached between the British Governor Van Batenburg and Governor Frederici of Surinam for the "adjustment of the differences with respect to the correct boundary between the two colonies."[2] Under the terms of the Agreement, the Corentyne River was to serve as the dividing line between the two Guianas. However, regardless of this written agreement, it is difficult to say precisely where one state ends and the other begins. It is reported that the Agreement has been interpreted in such a manner that the Corentyne River is now owned by Surinam and that the water level of the river, which is subject to daily upstream and downstream movements of the tides, determines the perennially fluctuating boundary line of Berbice along the left bank of Corentyne. Two markers, installed along the west bank of the river, explain the claim of the Surinam Government over the Corentyne waters. One is located at the mouth of the river near Village 63 and the other is placed

---

1 Robertson Island, Melannan Island, Jackson Creek, Parrot Island, Little and Big Baboon Island and the Three Sisters Island to name a few of the many islands.
2 For details on the nature of the conflict and the transactions between the two governments on the territory of Berbice, see Clementi (1937: 65-79).

about 400 miles upstream at the source of the Kutani, a tributary of the Corentyne. It is here, just 40 miles from the Brazilian border that the river starts its course on a high hill and flows down to the sea. In the absence of proper border patrolling, these two markers, located at the extreme ends of the river, serve only as nominal indicators of the territorial claim of Surinam. In actual practice the waters of the Corentyne River are used mutually by both colonies, perhaps a little more by the Guyanese than by the people of Surinam. As will be discussed later, this shared traffic and regular contact through the river has added new dimensions to the community life in the Corentyne area. It has lent certain extra-insular factors which contribute to the development of extra-community dependencies and involvements.

**The Village Defined**

The village of Crabwood Creek extends over an area of some 4000 acres. It measures about two miles in length and three and a half miles in depth. A simple definition of the boundary lines of the village is not easily made and may often be misleading since the term Crabwood Creek is used administratively and otherwise in many different ways. The last population census of Guyana in 1960 (printed in 1965), while dividing the entire country into 1265 enumeration districts, has kept in view the matter of administrative expediency. Each enumeration district was kept within a workload limit convenient for a single enumerator. Thus in most cases, an enumeration district consisted of less than 200 households. In the census report Crabwood Creek has been demarcated as a large unit comprising 55 enumeration districts. Treated as such, the northern boundary of the village would be drawn along the drainage canal between villages number 51 and 52 (Corentyne, Berbice) and the southern boundary would be marked by the "side line" between grants No. 1779 and 4043. The concept of the areas to be included within the village of Crabwood Creek has never been so expansive. The census demarcation also fails to correspond either with administrative identification of the area or with the postal beat lines. For the purpose of the present study, the boundaries of Crabwood Creek have therefore been confined to the limits identified by the local community. As such, the present boundaries of Crabwood Creek are determined by the "side line" between Grants 847 and 1804 on the north, the "side line" between Grants 1779 and 4043 on the south, by the sea dam facing the Corentyne River on the east, and by the Crown Land on the west. This definition of the village incidentally avoids any adverse criticism of arbitrary selection since it agrees legitimately with its own administrative demarcation as a Local Authority.

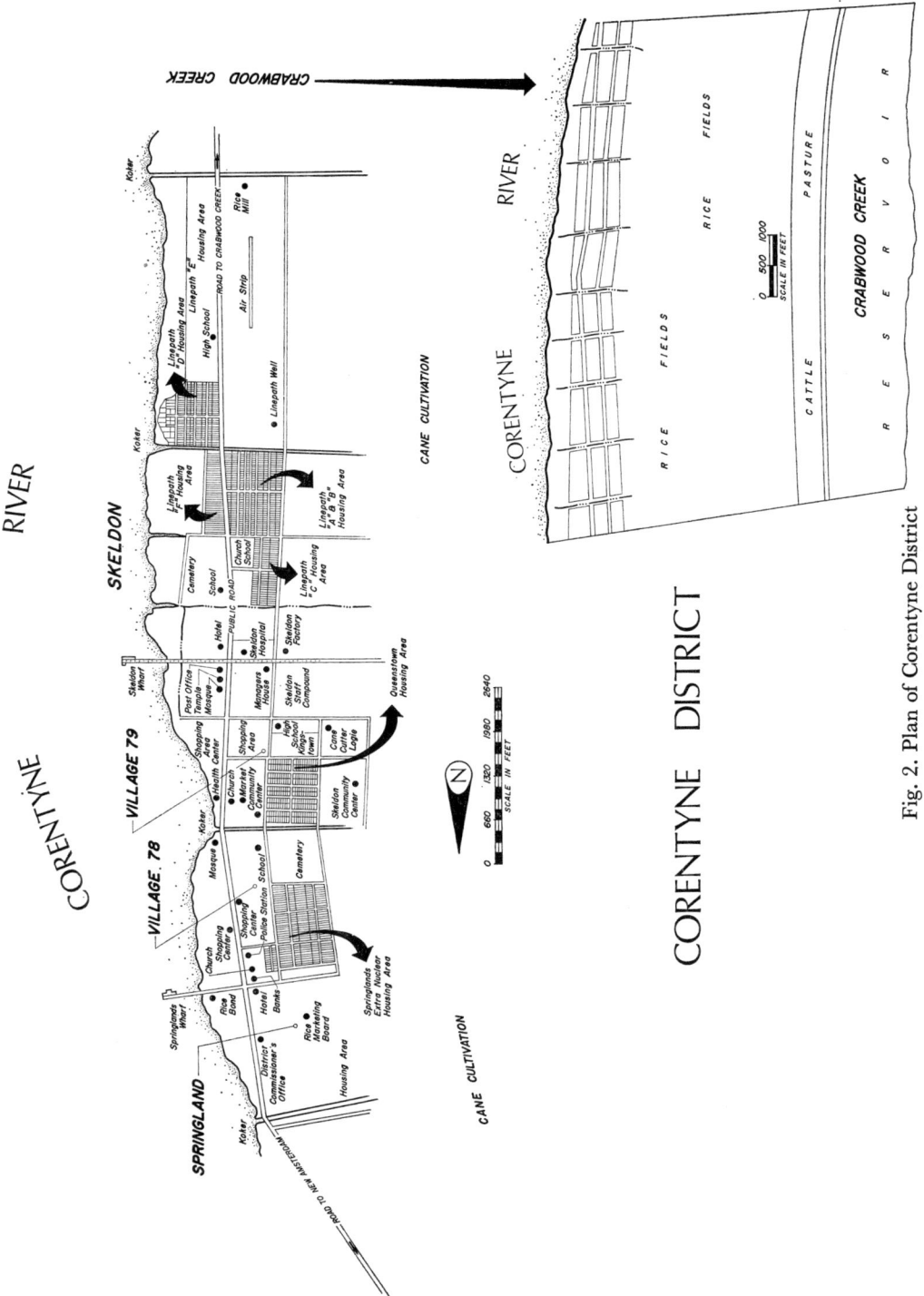

Fig. 2. Plan of Corentyne District

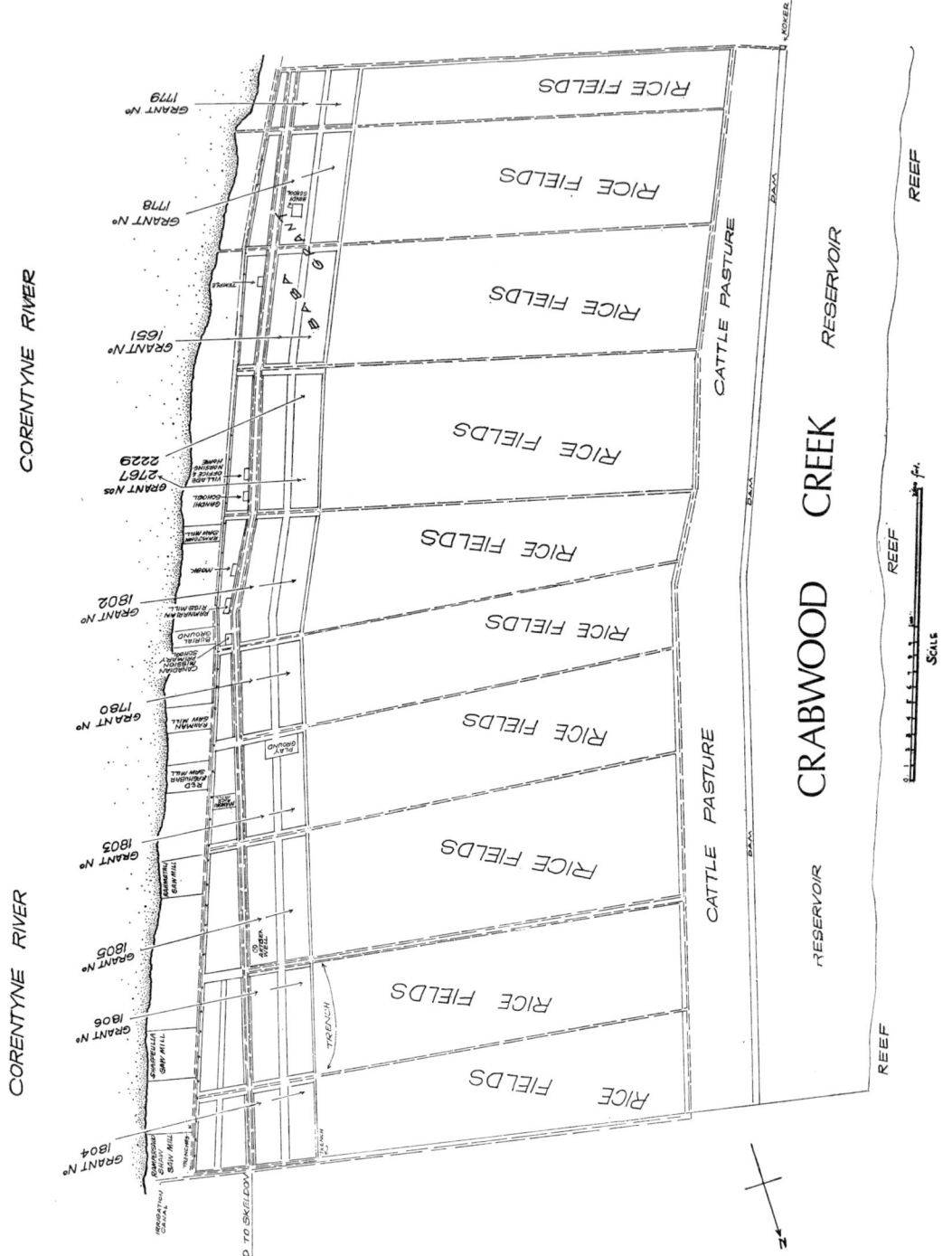

## Georgetown to Crabwood Creek

The journey from Georgetown to Crabwood Creek is time consuming and hazardous. For an ordinary traveler who does not own a car, various kinds of transportation are needed such as train, ferryboat, bus, taxi-cab, cycle and at times even a tractor ride to reach the village. To cover the total distance of 120 miles one has to count on spending seven or eight hours averaging, approximately, 15 to 18 miles per hour. If everything is functioning normally the railway trains leave Georgetown twice a day for Rosignol, a port town west of the River Berbice. The trains are slow, and it takes three hours to reach Rosignol. At Rosignol the passengers are picked up by a huge ferryboat which crosses the vast span of the River Berbice in about one hour and docks at New Amsterdam. A bus or half a dozen taxis wait in New Amsterdam for the arrival of the ferry. All of them carry passengers on the single public road running from New Amsterdam to Crabwood Creek. The bus stops at every village on the way and does not go beyond Skeldon which is two miles from Crabwood Creek. This final distance has to be covered on foot, or by cycle or tractor. Part of the journey can be speeded up if a person decides to travel by car, but the travel by car is generally avoided because the road conditions are extremely poor. Furthermore, the taxi fare is fairly high for an average man. Consequently most of the people travel by train. The journey is unpopular and is undertaken only when unavoidable. The following account typifies the reaction of a Guyanese when he is obliged to undertake the journey.

> Me (my) Lord when you a go da (that) side Skeldon you first take one car or taxi or bus or you taken um the train from des (this) side, then you go all the way that is if the rain na fall make um big hole, lots of water splashing the wind shield, tires get stuck, you go all the way to Rosignol at the ferry stelling. And from ferry stelling you cross over river and the river ya reachem da (that) side to New Amsterdam. Then from there you taken um car or taxi and you go, then scheuffer boi (boy) a preetty young and they tak care of you. Sometime it takem so long journey, take 7/8 hours. It is terrible Bhaiya (brother) to go from awee (our) side to Crabwood Creek. It takem lots of time you get tired, and you sit in the car and you get so tired to travel from des (this) side to da side.

## Growth and Formation of the Village

Crabwood Creek owes its name and origin to a creek which ran, years ago, through Grant No. 1802. Much of the creek has now been filled by a regular dumping of refuse and garbage by the villagers. A slight incline of the creek, however, survives even today, indicating its location in the past. According to folk traditions, not long ago the whole area was covered with an overgrowth of "crabwood" trees extending on both sides of the creek. The Indian indentured laborers ("Coolies") living on the adjoining plantation, Skeldon, met much of their lumber needs for house construction and kitchen fuel with the supply of wood from this area. Many senior citizens such as Haji Ramjohn (now living in Springland) still recall their early ventures toward the reclamation of this land. In fact, official records testify that the history of Crabwood Creek goes back "some one hundred years when a few adventurous people left nearby Skeldon, Springlands and adjoining areas to do logging and rice farming on lands, granted to them by the Crown, on long term leases.[3]" The first Grant was the same as the one that is now called No. 1651. Measuring around 100 acres, it was acquired by Ramnauth Maraj, a retired hand from the sugar plantations in Skeldon, for farming rice. To many of his friends and acquaintances Ramnauth's acquisition appeared to be a fruitless venture holding no promise for the return of his original investment, let alone of profit. However his early background in an Eastern district of Uttar Pradesh, India, where he had learned rice farming by helping on his parents farm, encouraged him to draw from his early experience and experiment with rice in Guyana. He went ahead with his scheme regardless of warnings and discouraging comments from friends. Shambhudat, the grandson of Ramnauth Maraj, still lives in the village and recollects the story of his grandfather which he heard from his father, Sewkumar, during his childhood. His account runs as follows:

> When me (I) was one small boy, me (I) used to hear Baap (father) talk of how me (my) grandfather gottum (got, this rice land ya (here). Baap tella (told) me that me (my) grandfather come from Bharat Mata (Mother India) long time ago, you know long time ago to come to cut sugar cane ya sa (this side) on Skeldon Estate. When me (my) grandfather retired from cutting sugar cane he gottum (got) piece land from government. This land ya (here) was lot of bushes, lots of tall trees like a forest. This then he cuttem down, he makum (made) nice for planting the rice. Rice cultivation, this now what he will do. Now when he startem (started) this rice cultivation, you know putum the irrigation allum of he (all of his) friends tellum (told) him na do da (don't do that). It no make him prosperity, it too much work, it nah (not) worth anything. They laughed at him, he nah (no) he go ahead. He plantum (planted) this rice. Was long time ago in the old country Bharat Mata (Mother India) when he was once small boy his papa used to plantum (plant) rice that side, little boy he learnum (learned) to plantum (plant) rice there. When come here he know how to plantum (plant) rice so like da (that) he started to plantum rice ya sa (this side).

Most of the early settlers of the village were retired Indian indentured laborers from the Skeldon Estate. They had worked strenuously on the estate as field workers and had saved as much of their earnings as possible with the hope of returning to India after the expiry of their contracts. The money was saved and their indenture period eventually expired, but their dream to return to India remained unfulfilled. Most of them stayed in Guyana and established villages such as Crabwood Creek.[4] Why did the Indian indentured immigrants elect to stay in Guyana instead of returning to their homeland? Shambhudat's account of his grandfather is extremely useful in providing an answer to the above question. He continued . . .

---

3 "Community Development Program Report," Ministry of Local Government, Social Welfare and Cooperative Development, Georgetown, Guyana, April 1956, page 3.
4 Data collected in 1960 indicate that this trend still continues (Despres, 1964: 1060).

Actually when me (my) grandfather had finished working on the estate and saved lots of money he wanted to go back home to old country. But when he came ya sa (here) a little boy and live on plantation he had to live in one house called "logie" where everybody of all Jati lived together. They eat, sleep and lived together. And so happened he met one girl from lower class-sudra and he married. Then they lived together and when come time to go home he had one big problem there, he married a lower caste, he could not keep up Dharma so when time to go India he could not go because his family da (that) side would not accept him there.

Crabwood Creek is perhaps one of the first places in Guyana where the East Indians applied one of their own historical-traditional patterns to community life. This pattern was translated into action in the form of mutual cooperative labor utilized to dig trenches for the irrigation of the rice fields and by the creation of a network of social institutions to support this economic base. The establishment of innumerable villages in India involves a meeting of the needs of the community through the cooperative efforts of one and all, within the framework of an aggregate of several families, approximating generally to an acceptable set of social norms, ethos, common cultural characteristics and values (Dube 1963: 202). The village of Crabwood Creek had a similar beginning. Different though it may seem in certain specific details, it retains certain cultural traits that it shares with its counterpart in India. This makes Crabwood Creek appear, in general, like a typical East Indian village.

The village of Crabwood Creek grew like a mushroom. At first there was no road, and transportation by small open boats on the Corentyne River was hazardous. As more and more people began settling in the area, however, the need for a road became imperative. In 1912-14, the newly formed community, on its own initiative, constructed a temporary road for establishing regular land communication with outside areas. This event is recalled by young villagers with a feeling of pride for the daring enterprise of their East Indian ancestors who applied their genius, unabated by hazards, to the opening of new sources for the enrichment and prosperity of the colony.

> You see des (this) village ya (here) was wan (one) big jungle. Awee (we) people have really put lata (lot of) work here. Them old people had worked hard and save their monie (money) which they get from working on the Sugar estate. De (the) land was very hard to work on. First most of the land was on lease from de (the) state. But awee (we) people who builum (built them) up like des (this). It is awee (we) people who put all these trenches for irrigation and awee (we) use them power pumps for pumping de (the) wata (water). It is awee (we) people who cut all de (the) big jungle. And so everybodi (everybody) worked elat (a lot) and buil up des (this) village ya (here). Then we buil (built) awee (our) houses, awee selves (ourselves), awee (we) put in roads and W.C. (bath rooms), awee (we) even get delco (dynamo) power and so awee (we) get electric light.

In 1926 the management of Skeldon, the adjoining sugar estate, took upon itself the conversion of the dirt road into a burnt earth public road as a measure to create better industrial relations with the populace. Later, in 1954, road was asphalted by the Government.

The economic pressures of World War II directed the attention of the administration to this otherwise unplanned growth of Crabwood Creek. During the war a gradual shortage of food was noted in the Caribbean area as a whole. Prompted by the need to step up food production, preferably from local sources, Crabwood Creek, with its self-activated human potential, attracted the attention of the colonial government. Governor Gordon Lethem, in the course of his visits to the area in 1944, made, with a minimum reluctance, the first free grant of three-quarters of a million dollars[5] for the development of this area. An amount of one half million was immediately invested in further reclamation of cultivable land, particularly for the construction of concrete sluices (*kokha*) to improve the community-built irrigation system. The remaining amount was spent on auxiliary projects to somewhat ease life in the community. The "self-help" spirit of Crabwood Creek with due monetary encouragement from the government brought well earned favors from the Governor. The "first depth" of land measuring 300 rods[6] eastward from the sea wall (Back Dam) is now owned, as a result, by people under "transport right." The rest of the land which includes two more strips of 300 rods each is held in annual lease at the nominal rate of 20c per acre for 21 years. This lease is extendable for similar periods for any length of time.

In many ways Crabwood Creek is not unique. Although it is a relatively new community, it is a village just like so many other East Indian villages in the lowland area along the coast. Life goes on here just as it does in other villages. The people live in the same kind of houses, have the same festivals and celebrations, go to the same places of worship and have the same type of elementary schools. One of the villagers observes this fact in the following words:

> Most of de (the) land is de (the) same lika des (this) ove (over) de (the) river dy (there) at Rosignol. Most a (of) de (the) house a (are) do (the) same, wood or some kancrete (concrete). Awee (we) have our celebrations, Phagway, Christmas, Eid, Roza and the festivals like other places, like Port Maurant and along the East Coast. Also awee (we) have churches, Matya (temples) and Jamats (mosques).

The selection of Crabwood Creek as a unit of study was prompted by the fact that it is an East Indian Guyanese village where elements of cultural continuity are transparent and can be observed and subjected to analysis in an attempt to formulate a working hypothesis for the continuity of Indian cultural identity. An even more important element in its selection was the fact that whereas in the social scene of Guyana, by and large, the overwhelming pressure of the "Plantocracy" and the government has tended to force the integration of diverse ethnic groups into a single society, Crabwood Creek has maintained the historical continuity of the Indian traditional system. Had Crabwood Creek been placed in a position of complete geographical isolation or had it been an independent socio-economic and ritual unit enjoying recognizable self-sufficien-

---

5 Community Development Program Report. Ministry of Local Government, Social Welfare and Cooperative Development, Georgetown, Guyana (April 1956, p. 3).
6 In Guyana a rod is measured as equal to 12 ft. or 4 yds.

cy, the phenomena of cultural continuity would hardly need explanation. However, such is not the case in Crabwood Creek. While the village does enjoy a partial isolation, it is also well connected with extra-insular relationships. The following brief resume will perhaps serve to delineate the extent of these relationships, and thus help to give a deeper appreciation of the process involved in the maintenance of cultural continuities.

Under East Indian stimulus, cane cultivation has been supplanted by rice farming. The tropical climate is warm and although near the equator, the heat is tempered by cooling trade winds. The climate is thus suitable for the cultivation of rice. Rice is grown for both subsistence and cash. Under a government regulation each farmer can keep only one bag of rice per month for his family. The rest has to be sold to the Rice Marketing Board for cash payment. The regional branch of the Board is located in Springland, a town about four miles from the village. At the time of harvest, when all the farmers are obliged to visit the Rice Marketing Board regularly, Springland becomes the meeting place of farmers from all the neighboring areas. Thus at this time of year Crabwood Creek becomes a part of an area of interaction with a radius of about 30 miles.

Although it is basically a rice growing village, farmers also raise cattle which have to be traded in the neighboring markets. This provides another source of contact with outside communities.

Another product of the area is lumber. Logging and sawmilling are therefore subsidiary industries which elicit regular contacts with major towns such as Georgetown and New Amsterdam.

Besides these economic factors there are many political and social factors that have contributed equally to the establishment of extra-insular relationships between Crabwood Creek and the outside community. Given the hazards and delays of travel between Georgetown and Crabwood Creek, and the limited means of communication which exist, one is likely to presume that the central authority of Georgetown would be thinned to a negligible degree when it reached the village. However this is not, in fact, the case as can be illustrated by the following example drawn from the political behavior of the East Indian community. A characteristic feature of the political affiliations in Guyana is that, generally speaking, the people of each ethnic group tend to belong to the political party of their own ethnic label. The transmission of the political messages of these groups and the formulation of their political response happens with an almost electrical speed, and the daily political developments and occurrences reach uninterruptedly to the inner core of each community. Evening assemblages of young and old, each reclining on the cemented sides of the sluices and discussing local politics until late in the night, are a usual sight. Political messages, when needed, are quickly passed from one "*Kohka*" assemblage to another by young political enthusiasts riding on cycles or on their tractors which are often substitutes for cars. Crabwood Creek thus does not stay as a backwater to the main political stream of the Central Government in Georgetown.

As stated earlier only one road runs along the coastal strip. Almost all the settlements are located on either side of this "Public Road" where they have relatively easy access to the cities. In this settlement pattern, the communities are connected continuously with only occasional intermittent gaps between New Amsterdam and Crabwood Creek. Thus intercommunity relationship, interdependence and mobility are quite extensive. Higher secondary schools, popular temples, mosques and churches, dispensaries, cinema houses, permanent wholesale and retail shops offering a wide range of articles, post office, hospital, police station, jewelry shop, and the weekly market place are all situated in villages No. 78 and 79 (see Fig. 2). Inhabitants of Crabwood Creek must, therefore, frequently and in many cases daily, cross the boundaries of the village to obtain services provided outside the village. On occasions such as marriage, Yagya, Kali Pooja, and festivals, intercommunity visiting is the normal routine rather than the exception.

One more important fact remains to be stated. The village, barring a few "dry goods stores", grocery shops and parlors, has no market of its own. Weekly visits to the neighboring markets are therefore a normal routine. Thus Crabwood Creek exists as a social nucleus where one can observe a constant human interaction on economic, political and social levels both within the unit and without.

**The Village Population**

Crabwood Creek, because of the history and nature of its growth, has come to be a homogeneous community of East Indians. More recently some members of other ethnic groups have entered the village and have established permanent dwellings, but the East Indians still form the core of the population.

In the Census Report, the village population has been classified under five ethnic categories: East Indians, Negroes, Mixed, Amerindians (American Indians), and Others. Whereas most of the terms are self-explanatory and indicative of ethnic origin, the category of "Mixed" is comprised of persons born of mixed parentage. Information from the Census Report of 1960 duly checked and updated by the writer with the help of local informants, the latest available records from the offices of the Registrar General, Immigration Agent General, and the Local Authority disclosed a total population of 3,090 persons living in 541 private households. Table No. 6 lists the population according to ethnic groups.

Most of the East Indians are descendants of the first village householders who, for most of their lives, had worked as laborers on the Skeldon Estate Sugar Plantation and had settled in the village when they left sugar estate employment. Some had come here from other areas such as Essequibo, where living conditions became harsh due to the decline of the sugar estates. Most of the new settlers were attracted to the village by the availability of land for rice cultivation and the proximity of the area to the timber belt from which the logs

THE VILLAGE OF CRABWOOD CREEK 51

Table 6
Ethnic Population of Crabwood Creek

| Category | Male | Female | Total | Percentage |
|---|---|---|---|---|
| East Indians | 1546 | 1439 | 2985 | 96.6 |
| Negroes | 33 | 18 | 51 | 1.7 |
| Mixed | 29 | 19 | 48 | 1.6 |
| Amerindians | 4 | 1 | 5 | .1 |
| Others | 1 | — | 1 | — |
| Total | 1613 | 1477 | 3090 | 100.0 |

of crabwood can easily be towed by boats down the Corentyne River. Of seven saw millers and two rice mill owners all except one have come from outside the village. All the local mills are owned by East Indians. They live in the village with their respective families, and also provide housing for the laborers' families working in the mills. Ninety-five per cent of the mill laborers are East Indians. Thus, movement from outside the village has not disturbed the ethnic composition of the village population.

Table 7
East Indian Population by Generation

| Generation | Male | Female | Total | Percentage |
|---|---|---|---|---|
| First Generation | 39 | 28 | 67 | 2.2 |
| Second Generation | 267 | 252 | 519 | 17.4 |
| Third Generation | 350 | 328 | 678 | 22.7 |
| Fourth Generation | 605 | 585 | 1190 | 39.9 |
| Fifth Generation | 275 | 256 | 531 | 17.8 |
| Total | 1536 | 1449 | 2985 | 100.0 |

Table No. 7 shows the generational strength and sex distribution of the East Indian population in the village. As will be seen in the subsequent pages of this study, an understanding of the generational classification of the East Indian population is extremely relevant for the purpose of my research. At this point, however, I will confine myself to a definition of the criteria used for classification.

The first generation is comprised of those East Indian immigrants who arrived in Guyana as indentured laborers. Some East Indians are reported to have arrived even after the termination of the Indenture System in 1917 on the invitation of their friends and relatives. Such people settled down in the Colony and worked as plantation laborers like the others. They have also been included in this category. In short, the category of the first generation immigrants includes all those who were born in India and arrived in Guyana as immigrants. There are 67 first generation immigrants in the village.

The second generation immigrants category is made up essentially of those East Indians who were born of East Indian parents belonging to the first generational category. It may be pointed out, however, that some persons placed in this category may have either one of their parents born in Guyana. The major criterion used here for defining this group is thus the birth of the person himself. The persons placed in the category of second generation immigrants were born in Guyana and were raised in the local environment of the Colony. The domestic environment in which they imbibed values and learned the ways of life was still not far removed from the traditional Indian pattern. Their parents spoke Hindi within the home and performed most of the rituals and ceremonies associated with the life cycle in traditional Indian style. It was only in their work situation that they had to communicate with others in a different language. In spite of their contact with members of other ethnic-racial groups, their lives revolved mostly around their own families and their own community. Close association between people of the first and second generation both at work and in homes, has contributed to the establishment of strong relationships between the two generations. Of the total East Indian population in the village 519 persons can be placed in second generation category.

The members of the third generation category were born of East Indian parents of Guyanese origin. Their knowledge of India is mostly derived from their parents who have themselves never seen the country. For this generation, India is a country that has been transformed from the world of realities to a land of fantasy. On finding that the investigator was born in India, one of the ladies inquired, "Is it true that Indian mangoes are four times bigger than our pumpkins?" Many of them have received education in schools run by Christian missionaries (mostly Canadian Mission Schools). They can understand Hindi, but find themselves more in tune with the local version of the English language, which they use in their daily conversation. They tend to participate more in the general life of the colony and are apt to relate their problems to the overall economic, political, and social trends of the colony. This group is comprised of 678 people and forms 22.7 per cent of the East Indian population in the village.

Members of the fourth generation are the offspring of third generation immigrants, and form by far the largest segment of the village society. Table 7 indicates that they form almost two-fifths of the village population (1190 out of 2985). People of this generation have almost completely lost comprehension of Hindi. Only a few words of the language are used in their vocabulary. These words pertain to areas of immediate concern such as Bhat (Rice), Roti (Indian pancake bread), Dhoti (Indian sari, an untailored piece of cloth wrapped around the body), Pooja (worship), Matia (temple), etc. Some major changes are noticeable in dress patterns which reflect a shift from Indian to European styles. Members of this group seem to be very aware of their Indian origin, but when the investigator asked the places from which their ancestors came to Guyana, or the names of their living relatives in India, they expressed total ignorance. Some replied in a rather irritated tone, "But why you ask, can't you see, awe (we) Indians." They wish to participate effectively in the social, economic and political life of the colony, but their mode of participation demonstrates a tendency towards cluster formation in order to keep themselves distinctive as a group. They tend to picture themselves as a more cohesive unit as compared to groups made up of other ethnic-racial stocks. "Awe (we) Indians are all like brothers, but they (Negroes) don't care for each other—son na (not) care for old man (father) and old lady (mother) and old man na (not) care to look after their picknees (children)." The spirit of mutual cooperation is looked upon as a way of acquiring a higher position for the East Indian community in the general Guyanese society. Many members of this category wish to excel over members of other ethnic-racial stock in education and leave the village to participate in the life in urban areas. They seek to acquire skills that could ease their adjustment in the urban environments of Georgetown. With this end in view, many of them have already acquired higher training or are planning to go to foreign countries such as Canada and England to acquire specialized knowledge in various professions such as law, medicine, dentistry, nursing and education, etc. Thus the goals of this group are more or less identical with the general goals of Guyanese society, but it should be kept in mind that these goals are perceived while maintaining their group identity. Members of the third and fourth generation have many things in common. Most outstanding among these is the tendency to perceive their ethnic problems with reference to the overall economic, social, and political situation of the country.

Members of the fifth generation are still in the stage of infancy. They form 17.8 per cent of the village population.

Since the village dwellers have either inherited their title to land from their ancestors or have established themselves more recently on new lands, they are actually able to trace their descent to the first title holder. Members of the first and second generation immigrants remember names of the places in India where their ancestral home was situated. Mr. Roop Singh, who is a second generation immigrant and works part time in the office of the Local Authority, having found that I was born in Uttar Pradesh, India, pointed out that his ancestral home was located in the same state at Fayzabad, and expressed the desire to have a map of India so that he could locate the home of his ancestors.

In a random selection of 50 households seven males and four females were found to be first generation immigrants from India. Most of the men had lost their wives. Some are living alone, but most of them are part of a joint family and maintain common residence with their family members. The oldest of all, Dwarka Maharj, is about eighty years of age. He came from India (Paraspur, P. O. Khaiburpoor, Thana Itikot, Gonda, Uttar Pradesh) in 1907 at the age of 22. He claims to be a member of the Brahmin (Misr) caste. He speaks chaste Hindi and maintains a small personal library of the sacred books of Hindu religion such as "Ramayana" and "Mahabharata." As stated in Table No. 7 there are 67 first generation immigrants in the village, but they are distributed all over the village and do not have the ingroup feelings which would lead them to maintain an enclave of their own within the village. Some members of the older generation recall that, formerly, a kind of fraternal relationship was maintained among the persons who came to the colony on the same ship. To describe this relationship they used the kinship term "Jahazi-Bhai" (brothers of the same ship) which cuts across all communal and socio-religious classifications such as the caste system. This relationship has now almost completely disappeared.

Negroes, who form 1.7 per cent of the population, are mostly village laborers. They live on daily wages as construction workers. Some of them are employed in saw mills at manual labor and draw weekly payments. A few own donkey carts and earn their livelihoods by transporting lumber from saw mills to the nearby construction sites. Some also work as domestic servants. The house of one Negro is a favorite after-sunset hangout of the East Indian youths. This house is known for a more "western" type of living and for a conspicuous feature of over-extended hospitality to the visitors, expressed through a usual offer of "rum" and intimate social contact with a group of young girls many of whom have an undefined relationship with the family head. Many Negroes live alone without a family.

Forty-eight persons (29 males and 19 females) belong to a category which is classified as Mixed in the Census Report. They are persons born of mixed parentage, mostly from East Indian-Negro mixture. Some are born of East Indian-Amerindian parents. In the village, children of such interracial mixtures are called "Doghula" (an East Indian word of Persian derivation used disparagingly for those who do not have "pure" descent. For instance, persons born of intercaste marriages in India are also called "Doghula"). In the East Indian society of Crabwood Creek where caste structure is fluid and the caste based services, statuses, and roles are also unrecognizable, the distinction between "pure" and "Doghula" is made on the basis of marriages between East Indians and non-East Indians. Children of East Indian parents, even if their fathers and mothers belong to different religious denominations are not labeled as "Doghulas". East Indians express strong disapproval of cross-ethnic sexual unions. Informants expressed the desire to see that their children are married firstly within their own religious group, and secondly to any East Indian regardless of caste or religious denomination. None entertained the idea of marriage with Negroes for whom the term "Kafir" (heathen) was used quite frequently. "Mixed" people are, therefore, treated as marginal to the main society.

Among the inhabitants of Crabwood Creek, Amerindians are lowest in number. They form only .1 per cent of the village population. One family of 3 work as "chawkidar" (guardsmen) in a saw mill. Two other individuals work as helping mates to East Indian logging gangs. Except for their work they do not maintain any accountable social relationship with the villagers. Their main reference group is that of the Arawak Indians who have a settlement about 50 miles upstream at Uriala.

The fact that almost 18 per cent of the village population is comprised of new settlers, of whom 3 per cent are foreign born, testifies that new settlers have been accepted by the village. They have been able to purchase property and even establish marital relationships with the village community. Among the new settlers the majority are the families and dependents of saw/rice mill-owners, owners of grocery stores and rum shops, and their employees. Persons placed in these categories have strong relations elsewhere. They tend to maintain social relationships with relatives, most of whom are outside the village.

The solid core of the village consists of the property-holding East Indian group who form 97 per cent of the total population. They have their roots in the village extending back, in some cases, to two, three, or four generations. They maintain social relationships within the group and know most of the members by name and family background. They participate in the day-to-day life of the village and associate with each other in religious rituals such as Phagwa, Ram Nawmi, Kali Puja, Yagya, the birthday of Lord Krishna, and in secular celebrations such as days of historical and national importance. Community development projects and political activities are carried on with equal interest. Outsiders are never rejected by the group although it can be noticed that some reservations are maintained against a person unknown in the village. As a matter of fact, all the social and religious festivities and celebrations are made conspicuous by the attendance of people from outside of the village. The tendency, then, is not to reject outsiders and thereby not to keep the village an insular community.

Of the East Indian group, the Moslems, who form 13.9 per cent of the total village population and 16 per cent of the East Indians, have an undercurrent of ingroup feeling. They own all the sawmills, one of the two rice mills, and most of the big grocery stores. Weekly congregations in the mosque at noon for Juma (Friday) prayers, are fairly well attended by males of all age groups, and function as a regular channel of face to face contact. Matters of communal interest are discussed and decisions are made as a group. Announcements of sickness, death, marriage, promotions in jobs, opening of shops, etc., are made at the altar by the "miaji" (minister) and elicit group response and participation. Attached to the mosque is a Madrassah where Moslem children receive lessons in the reading of the Quran, methods of prayer, and in Moslem conduct of life. This practice keeps the people in constant contact with each other and serves as an integrative element in the group. Regardless of an ingroup feeling, the Moslems in general, identify themselves as East Indian and maintain close ethnic ties with the Hindus. Social and cultural identification with the East Indian ecocultural system is expressed openly in public places, such as the mosque. Ethnic ties cut across communal lines. Intra-communal marriages between Hindus and Moslems are not rare. Two such marriages were attended by the writer during his field work. In one case the bride was Moslem and the groom Hindu. The other case was just the reverse, the bride being Hindu and the groom Moslem. Six other cases were recorded where Hindus and Moslems were living as married couples.

Since approximately 97 per cent of the village population is East Indian, my observations of the life in Crabwood Creek and the analysis of the sociocultural system in terms of continuity and change will be concerned mainly with the Indian society. Comparative reference will be made to the other ethnic groups whenever appropriate.

## The Village Setting

There is only one main approach to Crabwood Creek—the Public Road—which enters the village from the northwest and runs like a spinal cord through the center of the village residential area to its southeastern boundaries. Most of the houses are located on either side of this road, where they form tight clusters on both sides for the entire length of the village. Recently some houses have been constructed along the unmortared sidewalks which are generally called "side roads." These are the roads which have branches off the Public Road on the western side of the village. In addition, there are a few houses on the "back roads" which run parallel to the Public Road and form little rectangles when they join one "side road" with the other. The "side roads" and the "back roads" are not used extensively. They serve as a source of entrance to the dwellings, but most of the village activities and much of the daily business concerning every household are conducted by the side of the Public Road. The Public Road is busy with people going to and from the shops and other focal points during the hours when places of business are open. The Public Road is also the scene of most of the village economic transactions, social activities and religious celebrations. The village schools, shops, community center, dispensary, church, mosque, "matia" (Hindu temple) and the artesian well are all located by the side of the Public Road. For the manifold functions that it performs with reference to the total community life, the Public Road may be called an important integrative factor in the community. Even a casual visitor to the village would not fail to observe that a kind of general satisfaction is drawn by the village dwellers from moving and assembling on the road. This is done so frequently by all members of the community that it would appear that their presence on the road gives them a feeling of being an intimate part of the larger group. And, as an interesting coincidence, during late hours of the night when people retreat to their houses their places are taken over by the domestic animals and cattle. As in a typical village scene in India the Public Road becomes crowded by the presence of noisy dogs and "sacred" cows.

The Public Road as described above enters the village where it crosses a culvert and runs through the village for about two miles, where it ends. This distance from the culvert to the terminal point of the Public Road determines the width of the village. The breadth of the village is counted westward starting from the sea wall and goes, in terms of local measurements, approximately $4\frac{1}{2}$ depths deep into the interior until it reaches "back dam," the water reservoir. Each depth measures equal to 300 rods. The first depth, nearest to the sea wall, is held as transport land, over which the people have proprietary rights. This land can be transferred from generation to generation and is reserved for residential purposes. It is divided into house lots of different sizes and dimensions.

As a normal practice the front portion of the plot, lying nearest to the road, is used for the construction of the house, and the back yard is utilized as a kitchen garden. The second, third, and fourth depths are "Crown land"[7] held on lease of 21 years which is extended automatically on payment of the lease charges. These areas are all in rice fields divided into plots which are owned mostly by the village dwellers. The average holding of a farmer is 10 acres. The village records do not show any cancellation of lease on the basis of non-payment of dues. This is probably due to the fact that the lease charges are nominal (12 cents per acre). Thus in actual practice the lease land is no different from the land held in proprietary rights. Beyond the fourth depth lies a tract of land of 800 acres which is 150 rods in breadth and runs completely across the width of the village. This field is the pasture land. It is owned by the village as a collective property. A wire fence between the pasture land and the rice fields keeps the cattle from destroying the fields. The Local Authority is responsible for its maintenance and charges cattle owners a nominal fee for each head of cattle in order to meet the running expenditure. It is a fascinating sight to watch the village youngsters herding their cattle to pasture in the morning and back again late in the evening. During the night the cattle are left untied around the house.

The village amenities include an artesian well, a medical dispensary, a burial ground, two government primary schools (formerly run by the Canadian Mission), one private school, two playgrounds, facilities for public assistance, police protection, village shops, the Local Authority hall for small meetings and gatherings, religious edifices such as a Moslem mosque, a Hindu "matia" and a Christian church. The Government provides for the maintenance of the Public Road and the Local Authority takes care of irrigation and drainage canals.

## Houses

Although shelter and protection from the outside environment is the basic function of the house, it is also a convenient category under which many other facets of culture can be discussed. Among the East Indians of Guyana the extra-residential function of the house stands out even more prominently, because in terms of the continuing Indian tradition, the ancestral home is looked upon as a sanctuary second only to a temple (Prabhu 1958: 214-216). The ideal Indian house serves as a symbol for the prestige, harmony and unity of all its associated members. The social status and the traditional human qualities of an individual are, in part, rated according to the general appearance and maintenance of his family house.

All the houses in Crabwood Creek are set back about 20 feet from the

---

7 The "Crown Land" was held earlier on lease of 99 years. In 1957 the Jagan Ministry reduced the lease period to 21 years.

Public Road. A narrow drainage trench runs between the house and the road. The drainage trench is spanned by a plank bridge on big logs wide enough to permit passage of a motor vehicle or a tractor.

The residences are generally one story structures raised off the ground from about 9 to 12 feet (some even higher than this) to avoid the high water level or mud on the ground. It is not uncommon that during the rainy season the streets, paths, and grounds become a sea of mud. The superstructure of the house is raised on "blocks" (wooden columns) resting on a concrete raft foundation. At the calculated height "sills" (girders) are placed across the columns. This prepares the base on which the residential unit is to be built. An "upright" (wooden wall) roughly 9' to 10' high is raised around the girders on their supporting columns. The enclosure thus raised is then divided into bedrooms, kitchen, living room and corridors by erecting partition walls. On top of the "uprights" a flat wooden roof is laid, supported by rafters placed diagonally across the "uprights." The roof is covered by "zinc" (galvanized tin) sheets. At every stage of construction, braces are used to keep the structure erect. For additional strength "tenants" (socket joints) are put on all the joints in the sills and the uprights to keep the whole structure tightly fixed. The area underneath the house is usually kept leveled or plastered by soil mixed with cow dung. This is the place where children play their games. More often this space is used as an open garage for the household tractor. A pleasing sight, however, is that of a hammock hanging by the girders with a member of the household resting in it leisurely, a sight which may be taken to symbolize the slow yet peaceful and rhythmic pace of life in the village.

Most of the houses are wooden structures. Of the total of 549 houses in the village only 55 are made of concrete. In some the concrete work has been combined with the wooden structure. The lower portion of such houses, which is generally used as a kitchen, is made of concrete and the upper structure which contains bedrooms, living room, and store etc., is made of wood.

As mentioned earlier, houses are prestige symbols. It is, therefore, not uncommon that in order to acquire a higher social status people tend to spend an excessive amount of money on the construction of houses. Informants frequently pointed out that many person have borrowed money beyond their means and have consequently involved themselves in heavy debts just to satisfy their social aspirations.

Prestige motivation is often an impelling factor in raking competition between neighbors. Since cooperation, as will be shown later, is the basic theme of village life, competition on house construction is not looked upon with favor and is perceived as a superficial display of wealth. In the course of field work, many houses located in Grants No. 1651, 1778, 1893 and 1805 were specifically pointed out to the investigator as cases of undesirable competition. It was reported that the owners took heavy loans for the construction of these houses only in order to compete with their neighbors, and that they are now facing great difficulty in paying back their loans. This explains the imbalance in the statements of local informants, which kept the investigator confused for quite some time. Informants reported that there are 48 upper class houses in the village, each owned by an individual family. But when questioned as to the number of upper class families living in the village their count never rose above 19.

## Households

Before explaining the structure and composition of the households in the village a brief explanation of the terms to be used is in order.

a) *House*: The term house has been used to denote a structure of any description made of concrete, wood, or simply a thatched shelter meant for the purpose of living, regardless of its dimensions and the nature of relationships between the residents.

b) *Household*: In general usage this term is used interchangeably with the term "family" to mean persons bound together by ties of marriage and kinship. Here it has been used in a broader sense to mean "a local and spatial group marked by propinquity and need not be made solely of family members" (Bohannan 1963: 78). Thus members of the immediate family, relatives and/or other persons sharing the household arrangements are included as members of the household. Living together and sharing at least one meal have been used here as major criteria. Servants who sleep in, if any, are also included as members of the household. Ideally, the household has patrilineal continuity in which each generation is linked to the next in genealogical succession through the male line.

c) *One-Person Household*: This consists of a single person carrying on his or her individual household arrangements.

d) *Single-Family Household*: This term is used to mean a household as defined above which is comprised primarily of the members of a simple biological family, consisting of father and mother with unmarried children. Close relatives, such as a surviving parent of either husband or wife (usually husband's) or unmarried brothers and sisters of the husband may also be residing in this type of household.

e) *Multi-Family Household*: This consists of a household as defined above within which two or more families are dwelling. It may, however, include some individuals who are not members of any of the families identified with the household.

*Table 8*
*Households by Number of Persons Living in Households*

| No. of Persons | | No. of Households | Percentage |
|---|---|---|---|
| A. | 1 | 28 | 5 |
| B. | 2-3 | 132 | 24 |
| C. | 4-6 | 182 | 33 |
| D. | 7-13 | 207 | 38 |
| | Total | 549 | 100.0 |

Conforming as nearly as possible to the above definitions, Table Nos. 8 and 9, prepared on the basis of the records available from the Local Authority and duly checked, corrected, and updated with the help of a team of school teachers, whose unreserved cooperation has been of great assistance to the investigator in many ways, reveal some interesting living patterns.

*Table 9*
*Houses by Number of Rooms*

| No. of rooms | | No. of houses | Percentage |
|---|---|---|---|
| A. | 1-2 | 242 | 44 |
| B. | 3-4 | 254 | 46 |
| C. | 5-10 | 53 | 10 |
| | Total | 549 | 100.0 |

Table 8 indicates that category D which is made up of the households with the largest number of members (7-13 persons per unit) is also the category into which the highest percentage (38 per cent) of household falls. Another set of data, collected subsequently, on the type of household yielded evidence (Table 10) that 80 per cent of the households are single family households. It can thus be assumed that most of the large households are single family households. Table 9 showing the relationship between the number of rooms and the houses in the village indicates that the category of houses having the largest number of rooms happens to be the lowest (10 per cent) as compared to other categories.

The final analysis of the size and type of the household and the average number of rooms in the houses makes a prima facie case for two assumptions: a) the households provide a very high density of interaction among the members, b) lack of privacy in the household is caused by economic factors, or privacy within the household as understood in the western sense is not relevant in Guyanese East Indian culture. Since construction costs are low and land is cheap the latter assumption appears to be more acceptable.

*Table 10*
*Household Types by Number of Persons*

| Type of Household | No. of Persons Living In | Percentage |
|---|---|---|
| Single family | 2472 | 80.0 |
| Multi-family | 576 | 18.5 |
| One person | 28 | 1.0 |
| Other | 14 | .5 |
| Total | 3090 | 100.0 |

Table No. 10 shows that two types of households bearing contrasting features are most frequent in the village. One is the single-family household and the other is the multi-family household. With 80 per cent of the people living in single-family households and only 18.5 per cent living in multi-family households, it is immediately apparent that single family households are more common than multi-family households. A general survey of the households in the village lends further support to the foregoing conclusion when it is found that of the total of 549 households, 445 are single-family households. They account thus, for 81 per cent of the households in the village. It should, however, be remembered that single-family households are not identical with nuclear families. Most of the single family households in Crabwood Creek no doubt center around a conjugal family, but, following Fortes, the formation of the unit of conjugal family does not represent the phase of "fission" marked by the break of ties with the family of orientation. On the contrary, it exists as a bridge between the phases of "expansion" and "replacement" in the "Developmental Cycle of the Domestic Group" (Fortes 1962: 1-14). By keeping either of the surviving parents and/or the unmarried brothers and sisters in the household the conjugal family in Crabwood Creek maintains both vertical and horizontal ties within the kin group and eases the transition when eventually one household expands into many households. It can be seen that the relationships between households are structured along kinship lines. In some cases relationships between the households of near kin are so close that the households can be described as supra-households whose members inhabit different houses.

**Household Hierarchy**

The household constitutes an immediate and long lasting social commitment for all of its members. Relationships between its members are governed by an order of privileges and obligations. The status and role of each person is well defined. It may appear on the surface that some statuses in a multi-family household, such as that of the brothers' wives in relation to their mother-in-law or father-in-law are equal, but strictly speaking no one in the household has his social equal. Each household has a hierarchical pattern of status organization and this status is not achieved by personal merit. Two main principles govern the hierarchy: males are superior to females and elders are superior to juniors. As a result of the patrilineal continuity of the household the above mentioned principles tend to be slightly modified giving rise to a corollary: the members related through the male line take precedence over their counterparts in the female line. This principle may not always be operative; other factors such as the nearness of someone to the household members, even when the person involved belongs to the female line, may alter the picture. Since the status of each individual in the household is ascribed, status awareness and sensitivity is developed from the very earliest years by way of active daily routines such as methods of feeding, mode of address and use of politeness in speech. Males eat first, and while they eat, females are required to check to see if they wish second helpings. When the elders are eating the younger ones are expected to serve them water. If anything is needed during meals and if the young ones are eating with the elders, it is the duty of the young ones to leave the table and serve the elders. The housewife usually eats last, alone in the kitchen after everyone is through and she is satisfied that nothing else remains to be done. The younger ones are not supposed to address the elders by name; they are required to use kinship terms. The elders address the younger ones by their respective names. The following description of a Crabwood Creek East Indian family will perhaps serve to give further insight into the subtleties of the household hierarchy.

    Ramnarain Mattai lives in a joint family household. He is 40 years old and his wife is 38. They have eight children; the oldest is a boy of 13 years and the youngest, a girl born only a few weeks ago. Ramnarain's younger brother, Anandnarain Mattai (32), still unmarried, lives in the same house. Ramnarain's father died five years ago. When alive, he was the head of the household, and Ramnarain and his family lived with him as did his other sons. The oldest brother, Roopnarain Mattai, moved out of the house with his wife and children because of a "minor issue" between his wife and his mother. He has constructed a house across the street on a family plot. After the death of the father, Ramnarain, being the oldest male left in the house, became the head of the household. His "old lady" (mother) is 55 and lives with Ramnarain as a member of the household. Ramnarain's younger sister is married outside of the village. She lives with her husband and children in village 64.

    The Ramnarain house has three rooms constructed in a row and a kitchen projecting at right angles at the end of the last room. A little open space (10' × 8') facing the front room is used as living and dining area.

    Ramnarain, his wife and 4 little children sleep in the front room. The next room is used by his younger brother, Anandnarain, and the two older children share this room with him. The third room is generally occupied by the "old lady." She sleeps in her room with two of her favorite "picknees" (little children). She says that she "likes all of them equally" but the reason why the same two always sleep in her room is that "they like her more than others."

    The Ramnarain family lives mainly on the income from a $21\frac{1}{2}$ acre rice field of which 14 acres belong to Roopnarain and Anandnarain. The net income is shared equally after all the expenditures are deducted. Besides the share in the rice field, Ramnarain owns 10 heads of cattle, 17 chickens and fowls, two goats and six ducks. After domestic consumption the extra milk is sold to the milkman from Skeldon. This adds to the daily income of the household. Anandnarain helps in farming, but twice a year; a) June through August, when the rice field does not require many hands and b) November through January, when the land is left idle after harvest for recuperation, Anand goes to the timber belt with a gang of 5 or 6 people for logging. Anand's income from logging is his own. He contributes a part of it to the household expenses, gives some to his mother, and saves the rest for his marriage.

    The "old lady" owns a tractor which her husband left behind as her exclusive property. She allows the tractor to be used for the rice fields of all of her sons and thus keeps the family held together on good terms. Although she lives mostly in Ramnarain's house, and all her belongings are kept there, she visits Roopnarain's house or her daughter's family in Village 64 regularly. Quite often she sleeps with them for days on end.

    The "old lady" commands respect from all. She is addressed as "mata," "maiyya," "old lady," or "Dadi" by the respective members of the household. She issues instructions to her daughters-in-law and supervises the house chores. The daughters-in-law avoid speaking to their husbands in the presence of the "old lady" as a sign of respect. She retains affectionate relations with her sons and her grandchildren.

Ramnarain is the son of the "old lady," but, as mentioned earlier, being the oldest male he is the head of the household. It is he who carries the greatest overt authority, prestige and responsibility. He enjoys ultimate power over the household organization, budget and co-residents' behavior. Even the "old lady" is supposed to consult him in all her extra-household relationships. As the main custodian of the household's welfare, his relations with other members are marked with reserve and lack of intimacy.

Ramnarain's wife is the housewife. She carries the entire burden of housework, besides helping her husband in the field. Her authority is lower than her mother-in-law's, but her position as mother as well as housewife often brings much behind-the-scene managerial authority. She takes care of the guests, guides the children and manages a great deal of the budget by keeping the purse for her husband. She is addressed by Anandnarain, her brother-in-law, as "Bhauji," a kinship term whose use is accompanied by a unique combination of joking behavior and respect.

Anandnarain's position in the household is rather nebulous. As the second oldest male in the household he enjoys prestige among outsiders and affection not unmixed with respect inside the household. Nevertheless, he has to maintain his position in constant balance with his older brother Ramnarain, the accepted head. His share in the rice field and individual earnings from logging grant him economic security and an independent position, but he cannot avail himself of his independence fully without earning social disapproval. This position makes him placid and unaggressive. He is addressed as "Bhaya" by his sister-in-law and "chacha" (uncle) by Ramnarain's children.

## Clothing

The clothing worn in the village of Crabwood Creek demonstrates the blending of two basic styles. One is a modified version of European dress, which in the context of the Caribbean area may more accurately be designated as Creole dress, and the other is the traditional Indian costume. The everyday dress of a Guyanese East Indian male is comprised of a pant, shirt and a felt hat with an occasional addition of a scarf around the neck. Shirts are more often worn hanging outside of the trousers unless a formal occasion evokes a sensitivity on the part of the persons involved to show themselves properly attired.

The female dress is again a blend of the two styles. It is comprised of a long baggy dress which normally hangs loose from shoulder to knee and a headdress made of madras cloth in a check design. Many females are seen in petticoats with a camisole-like dress hanging loose from the shoulders to cover the upper part of the body. This short dress is not meant to display the body or accentuate the contours. On the contrary, it tends to conceal the details of the figure and tones down its intimate definitions. Very few females are to be seen without a headdress. The older females are especially particular about covering their heads no matter where they are or what they may be doing. They can be seen wearing their madras headgear at all times, whether working in the rice fields, fishing on the riverside, attending social and religious gatherings or fixing food in the kitchen. A factor of relevance here is, of course, the traditional Indian practice in terms of which the use of a cap or any other form of head covering is not only regarded as a sign of reserve or retraint around the youngsters, or a show of respect to the elders, but also carries symbolism for both Hindus and Moslems. While offering prayers in the mosque or performing

"Puja" in "Matia" individuals of both faiths tend to cover their heads. To uncover the head in public is an index of westernization and is often looked upon by the old ones with distaste and disfavor. Occasionally even an attribute of shamelessness is attached to the girls who do not observe this practice.

Simplicity in dress is a traditional Indian virtue and is believed to reflect, to use a Gandhian mystical phrase, "the inner man," who according to Gandhi is essentially unostentatious, honest, and virtuous as opposed to being showy, exhibitionist and cunning (Dube 1955: 182). By any assessment, the dress styles in the village have changed from the traditional Indian "dhoti-choli" ensemble to a more western type of dress, but the continuity of the tradition of simplicity seems well pronounced among first and second generation immigrants. This continuity is reflected by their retention of traditional items such as the headdress and also by their use of subdued colors in clothing. A change in dress styles is especially noticeable in the younger generation. Brightly colored skirts and blouses are popular among the girls and so also are carefully pressed and matching arrangements of pant, shirt and tie among the boys. The girls also lean more toward individual hair styles rather than toward the traditional practice of covering their heads. As an excuse for their shift away from traditional styles, examples of Indian film stars are cited and their fashions are used as acceptable models of Indian tradition.

In short, a fairly distinct line can be drawn between first and second generation immigrants and their offspring forming the third and fourth generations in matters of clothing styles and personal adornment. This change can be explained in terms of functional adaptations of the East Indians to the dominant Creole culture. When questioned about this major change in dress styles informants offered a rather defensive explanation. One of them stated that in the "old days" men and women worked together in the weeding gangs. The trenches in which they had to work were sometimes breast deep and at other times shallow, but in any case, the females had to lift their "dhotis" before they entered, and so they had to tell the men, "Brother hide your face that we may pass." Gradually the unwieldy "dhotis" came to be replaced with the knee high dress which allowed more ease of action in the trenches. Work under these conditions was deeply resented and was considered an encroachment upon female chastity. Consequently one of the leading Indian national leaders, Mrs. Sarojini Naidu, in the year 1917 exclaimed in anguish, "Arise ye sons of Bharat Bhavan and extinguish the funeral pyre of immigration and save the chastity of women on the Sugar Plantations" (Anonymous n.d.: 9).

When the women dress for special occasions one can notice a combination of riotious colors which do not necessarily demonstrate a sense of harmony. Emphasis on the display of colors as well as the styles in dresses on the occasion of marriage ceremonies and social gatherings will be discussed in detail elsewhere. Suffice it to say at this point that in marriage gatherings and other social functions the choice of brilliant colors in dress is more than common. As suggested by informants such gatherings may also be looked upon as occasions which provide people an opportunity for the choice of future life partners. Bright and lively colors are worn by girls of marriageable age, in part to attract the attention of young men attending marriages. This information finds support in an interesting incident. Once while accompanying a village peddler of textile piece goods, I noted that the peddler's most effective sales pitch was one in which he referred to some forthcoming marriage event and suggested to the prospective customer that she purchase a brightly colored piecegood for a dress for her daughter in order that her daughter might look "distinctive" at the gathering.

Even a most conservative estimate of an average family's assets would lead one to believe that most of the families can afford to provide footwear for their children, as well as for the other members of the family, but it is more than common that school children are found without shoes in their classrooms. The number of barefoot children is definitely out of proportion to the number of families who can afford such expenses. It is also usual that the older members of the group often walk barefoot about their neighborhood. This very casual attitude toward footwear may be accounted for in terms of adjustment to local climatic conditions and geographical environment. More meaningful than this, perhaps, would be for one to note the striking similarity between the attitude of a village dweller in India and that of his counterpart in Guyana. In Indian villages the use of footwear is not common. More often than not, the use of footwear by anyone is considered an indication of his participation in a special ceremony.

CHAPTER SIX

# The Economy and Daily Life

THIS CHAPTER is devoted mainly to the description and discussion of the economic structure of Crabwood Creek. The study of the economic aspect of the village is intended to provide an additional insight into the way of life of the people. It is neither intended, nor required for the purpose of this study to go into greater details of the mechanisms of production, consumption, distribution and exchange. To be explicit, the presentation of the way of life and the relations which are entered into by the members of the village, both inside and outside of the community, as a consequence of their economic activity will remain the prime focus of discussion. This is appropriate since it has a direct bearing on the controversy over the relative usefulness of either the plural or the consensual model.

The economy of the village is primarily based on agriculture. The process of agriculture attends to the explanation of relations among the members of the family on one hand, and between the categories of persons such as landowners, tenants, agricultural laborers and various occupational groups on the other. In addition, the process of agricultural production and the government controlled system of distribution is in itself dependent upon the relationships which frequently cut across the boundaries of the village. Thus it will be seen that occupations, economic activities and social relations intertwine with one another.

With agriculture as the main support of the village economic structure it was expected that a high degree of homogeneity in occupations would be found, however this assumption proved to be untrue. As a matter of fact a wide variety of occupations such as logging, fishing, plantation labor, transportation, sawmilling, carpentry, animal husbandry, service, shopkeeping, exists in the village today. Some of these occupations are only recent additions. In spite of their heterogeneity, however, they have all tended to acquire a form of contractual character. It will be understood from the following description and discussion that although the people are involved in diverse types of occupations, agriculture still remains a basic part of their economy.

## Occupations

The occupations in the village can be roughly classified into four categories: occupations deriving principally from village agriculture; occupations deriving from the sawmilling industry: occupations related to transport and communications; and occupations derived from individual skills, carpentry, building construction and seasonal employment on the sugar estate in Skeldon.

*Farming and Agriculture.* Population statistics indicate that out of the 3,090 people in the village 2,504 are over ten years of age. When all of these are included in the category of "working group" this category accounts for approximately 81.2 per cent of the population. The age of ten can be used arbitrarily as the dividing line between "working" and "non-working" people because Crabwood Creek is essentially a small farming community and children of both sexes of this age or over, help older family members in the rice fields or in other economic activities related to farming. Such is not, of course, the universal practice. Some parents would rather see their children attending schools than spending time in the fields. The participation of children in the parents' occupations is thus only partial and is usually non-obligatory. During harvest time, when the paddy is processed in the rice mills, the children perform various light duties. No payment is made for their services but their participation adds indirectly to the family income. If the youngsters do not help at this time, the family will have to employ hired laborers, and the family income will thus be reduced by the amount of the wages paid. School authorities report that general attendance, especially in the upper level classes, usually drops at this time of year. If this voluntary element of the labor force is excluded, the actual working population of the village consists of only 1,505 persons (773 males and 732 females). Of this total 55.2 per cent are engaged in agriculture either as farmers, tenants, or agricultural laborers. This makes farming by far the most popular occupation of the village. It also happens to be an occupation in which females are active participants. Farming has some unique advantages over other occupations. Due to the seasonal nature of rice cultivation, Crabwood Creek farmers have time to supplement their incomes by engaging, if they so desire, in other economic activities such as fishing and logging. It is not uncommon that during the idle period young farmers and agricultural laborers hire a boat and go in groups "up the river" (Corentyne) to cut logs from the timber belt. Such expeditions last for weeks, even months, if the group is large and sufficient transportation facilities are available. When the males are away cutting logs, the females form small congenial groups of three or four in number and go to the riverside to catch fish, an important part of their every day food. "Hassa," a sweet water fish, is treated as a delicacy; "Houri" and "Yaro" are next in the order of preference. The morning and afternoon fishing routines, besides adding variety to the diet, provide a social outlet for the females. Family feuds, village problems, marriages, births, and other activities in the village are discussed during these fishing trips.

*Dairying and Animal Husbandry.* Dairying and animal husbandry have never assumed the position of full time occupations, but they exist as sources of supplemental income. In addition to providing a side income for the owner, the possession of cattle serves another purpose. It is commonly held that "if a person owns 15 head of cattle he owns a tractor." The credit facilities at the village shops increase in proportion to the number of cattle a person owns. On the average, a cattle owner will have somewhere around 5 to 10 head, but the largest pen in the village has about 100 cattle. The second largest pen has 60 head.

Three different breeds of cattle are found in the village:

1. Imported breeds such as Holstein, Zebu, and Red Pole yielding 8 to 24 pints of milk per day, depending upon the age and the health of the animal.
2. Creole breed yielding 2 to 8 pints per day.
3. Mixed breed (mixture of the imported and local breed) yielding 6 to 16 pints per day.

The cows are milked twice, once in the morning and again in the evening when they return from the pastures. Since little care is taken to improve the health of the cattle, the average yield of milk is very low. Much of the milk is used by local residents to meet their domestic requirements. The surplus is sold to the milkmen from Skeldon who visit the village daily and collect milk from door to door for nine cents per pint and then sell it to their buyers in the Skeldon area at twelve cents per pint. For the village people the "milk man from Skeldon" is not only a buyer of milk he is also a carrier of news and a person through whom messages may be sent to relatives and friends in Skeldon.

In line with Indian traditional and religious belief, the cow is considered to be a sacred animal, and except for Moslems and Christians no one eats beef. People of the older generation would hesitate to sell a cow to the butcher, but the younger generation tends to rationalize the sale, especially of old cows, by saying that it is better to sell them and get money for a worthy cause such as a girl's marriage or the performance of religious rituals, than to let the cow die on the road. While sitting in the house of an East Indian informant, the investigator once witnessed the sale of a cow. The old mother and the older brother opposed the transaction, but the younger brother argued strongly and convinced them in favor of the transaction by saying that the money from the sale could be spent on the "yagya" which the family was planning to hold the following month. Goats, sheep and chickens are raised by most families, and are used for food by almost all of the people.

*Sawmilling and Logging.* The occupation second in order of economic importance is sawmilling. Seven sawmills are already in operation within the village, and because of its nearness to the timber belt the village has even better economic prospects in sawmilling. A new sawmill is being established adjacent to the southern boundary of the village. Sawmilling is more or less exclusively an adult male occupation. Very few females or children are seen participating in sawmilling or the subsidiary occupation of logging. Of the total regular working population of the village only 14 per cent are engaged in sawmilling and logging as their exclusive occupation. This percentage, as mentioned above, tends to increase during the idle period of farming (May through July) when the village farmers engage in logging to supplement their income from the land. Such ventures are being encouraged by the sawmill owners. Prospective seasonal loggers are given provisions and groceries in advance, sufficient to last for the period they work in the forest. The adjustment of this advance payment is made when the loggers return to the mill and sell their logs to the sawmiller. Because of this advance the sawmiller can usually squeeze the loggers and expect a favorable price from them in these transactions. It is hard to determine in what proportion the Crabwood Creek sawmills contribute to the lumber needs of the colony, but the amount of lumber observed to have been moved to the different parts of the area lying east of the river Berbice is suggestive of the fact that the major proportion of the regional needs is met by the output of the Crabwood Creek mills. Sawmilling is rated as a lucrative business, and sawmillers enjoy a very high status in the village social hierarchy.

*Transportation and Communication.* The occupations related to transportation and communication are mainly an outgrowth of the sawmilling industry. The lumber produced in the village sawmills is transported to the neighboring areas on donkey carts. Since sawmills remain in operation all year round and lumber has to be moved out of the mills regularly, transportation as a regular occupation has attracted some people. Even though this occupation is not very lucrative it does provide a steady income to those involved. In all, 5 per cent of the actual working population are involved in transportation. This figure includes persons who own taxis and use them for commercial purposes.

*Other Occupations.* All other village occupations such as tailoring, carpentry, construction, shopkeeping, and leather and metal work are derived from individual skill. It is difficult to establish whether any of these skills are used as a regular source of income. Most of these crafts, except shopkeeping, attract customers only periodically. This hardly provides a basis for making use of these skills as a full time occupation. As such, individual skills are used periodically to supplement the regular source of income of the household mainly derived from agriculture.

Some of the inhabitants of Crabwood Creek earn their livelihood by working on the sugar plantation in Skeldon. Very few of them, however, have year round plantation employment. Most are employed only during the "grinding" season. This is the time when the sugar factory operates round the clock and the labor force is almost double its normal strength. Many kinds of odd jobs are done at this time such as dusting the cane to kill insects, catching rats in the field, digging and clearing the land for the next crop. Such jobs are called "tasks" and are paid at differential rates according to the nature of the work. Most of the "tasks" are done by males even though females are not completely excluded. Females are usually employed as water carriers to supply drinking water for the drivers and other laborers working in the field. However, there is a general feeling in the village that to work at a "task" is to expose oneself to the possibility of sexual advances by the supervisory staff. Most females, especially those of the younger age group, would rather stay home than work on the plantation if they can afford to do so. One of the many female informants who have worked on the plantation in the past stated:

> Bhaiya (brother), life en (in) des (this) plantation work ya sa (this side) is too much hard, but because of money situation and to keep awe (our) family from starving me got to workam (work) all day in this sugar field. When me work ya sa (this side) the man in

charge try to make fresh with me and do him favor, but des a na (this is not) what we bin (have been) taught a house (in our homes). Awe (our) Dharma (religion) will not allow such thing to happen; and when de (the) head-man takam (takes) any advantage awe (we) have no one to complain to and getam (get) justice. Awe (we) women prefer to stay a (in) home and takam (take) care of awe (our) picknees (children).

## Rice Cultivation

Rice is the main agricultural crop, and the economy of the village is essentially based on the cultivation of paddy and its conversion to rice. A brief description of: (a) methods of rice cultivation in historical perspective, (b) of participation of various members of the family at different stages of cultivation, (c) of annual cycle of activities, and (d) of the assessment of the average income derived from this source would be appropriate here because the coverage of these dimensions of the main economic activity provides insights into more than one area of village life. It reflects the nature of some of the adaptations that East Indians have made in Guyana. It further explains the pattern of relationships among the members of the family, the division of labor between males and females, and the basic level of their subsistence. More importantly it illustrates how the East Indian group developed a strong cohesiveness during the first and second generations, and when the population grew out of proportion to the productivity of land how they adopted new means of subsistence in the form of alternative occupations.

In an agricultural society it is not uncommon that the members of a family are held together by the joint possession or use of land and agricultural tools and implements. They function as a corporate unit in which each member contributes his labor according to his skill and capacity and shares the output according to his needs. When the group outgrows the sustaining power of the land the family unit, using land as the first base of subsistence, searches for alternative sources of living.

The discussion of rice cultivation that follows illustrates how the East Indians in Crabwood Creek first developed a well integrated and strongly cohesive society based on agriculture and subsequently adopted other occupations under the pressure of increased population. This phenomenon of the diversification of occupation appeared in Crabwood Creek preeminently at the level of the third and fourth generations. Rice cultivation is an East Indian innovation in Guyana. Most of the East Indian indentured laborers came from areas in India such as the eastern part of Uttar Pradesh, Bihar and Madras which are known for their rice production. It is not surprising, therefore, that

> when they [East Indians] were laboring on the coast's sugar estates they were encouraged by the owners to sow small paddy patches near their dwellings to aid subsistence, and they thus became the first rice planters on the Essequibo Coast (Skinner 1955: 24).

This statement also holds true for the rest of the country.

In former days, the rice cultivation process was similar to that practiced in

India. Oxen and the single-bladed iron plough were used in clearing and turning the soil. A small flat board was used for smoothing the "bea pond" for planting. The reaping was done by "cutlass." Thrashing was done by turning the oxen around an upright stake to which they were tethered. The paddy stalks were spread around the stake and the grains were loosened by trampling.

There was a clear division of labor between men and women in this work. The work with oxen and the plough was done by men, while women did the planting and transplanting of seedlings. The reaping, drying and threshing was done by all the members of the household. Many members of the community recall that the old system of rice cultivation continued in Crabwood Creek until ten years ago. At that time almost 90 per cent of the farmers still used this method. In the early 1950's the government induced farm machinery firms to sell tractors to the farmers on easy installments. The firm offered the sale on terms that included 1/3 of the cost (G.$4000.00) to be paid in advance and the remaining 2/3rds to be paid within two years in two equal annual installments. Knowing the benefits of tractor farming, most of the farmers responded favorably to the change. The old method of cultivation has now been almost completely abandoned. At times when the land is soggy or when the use of tractors is uneconomical, ploughing is of necessity done by bullock. Such cases are, however, quite rare. The oxen and the plough have been replaced by modern tractors. Most harvesting is now done by "combines" and the paddy is converted into rice at the mills.

*Single Crop Economy.* Only one rice crop is produced annually even though the possibility of producing double crops is not completely ruled out in statements by informants. The single crop economy is explained in terms of the limited supply of water and the seasonal involvement of the local people in other subsidiary economic activities. An additional explanation can perhaps be found in the words of an informant who stated that the plot reserved for pasture is too small (800 acres) for the number of cattle in the village. As such it can not be used regularly the year round and must be left fallow for a period of time to recover from its depletion. After harvest during late September and October, the village rice fields are, therefore, opened to the cattle and used as pastures until the next sowing season in April/May. The single crop system thus makes it possible for the village to practice a lucrative subsidiary activity. The limitations of the irrigation system and the unpredictable supply of water may perhaps account for the single crop economy.

## Annual Cycle of Rice Cultivation

*Ploughing.* January through March is almost a dry season. This period is punctuated by occasional rainfall which makes the soil soft and favorable for ploughing. It is during this period that the farmers are seen busy ploughing their fields, either with their own tractors, or with those hired from their neighbors. The soil is raked; leveling is done and the field is prepared for sowing the seed during these three months.

*Sowing*. Much of the seeding is done during April/May; seeding is still the work of the females. Normally this is the most active and enjoyable time for the women. For most of the year they remain involved in their domestic chores. During this period they have a chance to go into the fields and enjoy the fresh breeze out in the open. Small groups of women are seen in the fields singing songs and "shying" (broadcasting) the seeds by hand. If the broadcast seeds do not grow well or the rains have flooded the field transplanting has to be done. This is a hard job. A nursery bed is prepared; the seeds are germinated; the seedlings are grown and finally the transplanting is done. The transplanting process requires the help of the males.

*Watering*. The rice fields are irrigated through a network of man-made canals and the supply of water is controlled through a drainage system. During the rainy season (May through July) the water is conserved in the reservoir situated west of the rice fields. A "khokha" of 12' × 12' in size operates here to regulate the supply of water from the reservoir to the canals. Each farmer then has his own "khokha" (8' × 7') by which the water of the canals is taken into the fields. When the required quantity is received and the rice plants are duly irrigated the water is drained out by another "khokha" (8' × 7') to a side line (drainage canal) which carries the water out to the river. The watering is done mostly during July and August.

*Drying*. Following the irrigation of the fields the farmers keep checking the growth of the rice plants. The load of work is reduced by a considerable extent at this time. Only weeding and dusting is done to protect the plants. A hot spell with sun is needed during late August and September for drying the rice fields. A wave of gloom prevails over the village when dark clouds form thick clusters over the sky and threaten a downpour of rain. Everyone looks concerned and downcast. No rituals are performed to urge the heavens for favors but the whole community plunges into an unending conversation about the weather and its possible adverse consequence. If everything goes well it takes three weeks for drying the crop.

*Reaping*. Late September, October and sometimes even the early part of November are spent in reaping the harvest. These are the busiest days for the village farmers. Almost all the members of the household are involved in one way or another. After the harvesting has been done the paddy is taken to the rice mill for processing. After processing, the rice is classified and poured into separate jute bags according to its classification. Once classified and packed the rice bags are carried from the mill to the Rice Marketing Board for sale. Most of the reaping is done by "combines." The farmers who have small holdings, however, find the use of combines to be uneconomical. They do the harvesting by hand. When the plot is big enough and the harvesting can be done by combine, it is both fast and economical because this process includes, besides cutting, the hauling and the meshing of the crop. The major advantage to the farmer, in the use of the combine, lies in the fact that it takes only one day to finish the whole job. The time saved can thus be utilized to do other kinds of work for additional income. For authors who explain the continuity of antiquarian methods of farming among Indian farmers in terms of their fatalistic attitude, it is interesting to note that when given the possibility of maximizing their incomes through subsidiary occupations, the East Indian farmers in Guyana are susceptible to change and accept mechanization and automation in the agricultural process.

In order to determine the average farming income of a household a table detailing the average income and expenditure for a model plot of one acre has been prepared. Since most of the farmers have adopted mechanization it has been assumed that the farmer has made use of tractors and other machinery. The total yield per acre of land ranges from 18 to 22 bags of rice paddy or 9-11 bags of processed rice. The average yield per acre is thus 20 bags of rice paddy or 10 bags of processed rice. Each bag of processed rice weighs 180 lbs.

The average landholding of the farmer in Crabwood Creek is 10 acres. Thus, based on the following calculations, the average annual income of the farmer from his rice field is G. $880.00. This income is far below the need of an average sized family or household in Crabwood Creek. Economic pressure has, therefore, resulted in the adoption of the following courses of action which also reflect three predominant trends in the village economy: a) increase landholdings by pushing back the line of timber, b) avoid fragmentation of holdings by binding the family or household together through the reinforcement of Indian cultural tradition and practices, and c) supplement their income by engaging in other specialized or unspecialized occupations. As was stated in the beginning of the chapter all these trends have contributed to the creation of a network of contractual relationships between different categories of people in the village. A person may have one occupation as his major source of income, but he tends to involve himself in other occupations in search of further means of support. Thus a farmer is not always only a farmer but, with the change of the season, he may also be a logger, a tailor, a carpenter, a fisherman, a landlord, and/or a hired laborer. Consequently many different kinds of economic activities overlap each other in the life of a single individual. This occupational symbiosis is reflected in the rituals, ceremonies and, more importantly, in the network of social relationships which will be discussed in the next chapter.

It is obvious, from the above description, that agriculture is the main basis of the village economy today. The changing patterns of the village economy, however, may be perceived from the attitudes of the younger generation. In a sampling of 43 members (27 boys and 16 girls) of the younger generation it was noted that no one expressed an interest in agriculture and rice farming. Among the male informants the preferred occupational aspirations were reported as medicine, engineering, seamanship and the Civil Service. Among the female informants the occupational choices ranged from medicine, nursing and dentistry to employment such as account clerks and air hostesses. This departure from the traditional occupations was explained in terms of the desire of the younger generation to participate in the larger society of Guyana and to compete with other ethnic and racial groups.

*Table 11*

*Average Expenditure and Income for a Plot of One Acre Yielding 20 Bags of Rice Paddy or 10 Bags of Processed Rice*

| Expenditure | |
|---|---|
| A. First ploughing or "cut" | G.$ 5.00 per acre |
|     Second ploughing or "cut" | 4.00 per acre |
|     Third ploughing or "cut" | 3.00 per acre |
| B. Broadcasting of seed or "shying"[1] | 1.00 per acre |
| C. Weeding[1] | 3.00 per acre |
| D. Dusting | |
|     1. cost of labor[1] | 3.00 per acre |
|     2. cost of insecticide | 3.00 per acre |
| E. Irrigation and control of water[1] | 5.00 per acre |
| F. Reaping, hauling and meshing (by combine) @ G. $2.00 per bag paddy | 40.00 per acre |
| G. Cost of transportation to rice mill | 5.00 per acre |
| H. Processing @ G. $2.00 per bag paddy[1] | 10.00 per 20 bags |
| I. Milling and grading of 10 bags of processed rice | 10.00 per 20 bags |
| J. Transportation | |
|     1. from the rice mill to Rice Marketing Board in Skeldon | 2.50 per 10 bags |
|     2. from Rice Marketing Board to Georgetown | 3.60 per 10 bags |
| K. Rates to be paid to Local Authority | 8.00 per 10 bags |
| L. Cost of bags | 6.00 per 10 bags |
| *Total* | G.$ 112.10 |

| Income | | |
|---|---|---|
| A. Extra No. 1 | 9 bags @G.$18.90 per bag | G.$170.10 |
| B. Broken rice | 1 bag @G.$ 8.00 per bag | G.$ 8.00 |
| *Total* | | G.$178.10 |
| Net Income (per acre yeilding 10 bags of processed rice) | | G.$ 66.00 |
| Income through savings if household helps with labor | | G.$ 22.00 |
| *Total* | | G.$ 88.00 |

1 These items of expenditure are usually done by the farmer and the members of his household. This adds G. $22.00 to the net income calculated above.

CHAPTER SEVEN

# Social Organization and Symbolic Systems

WITH ALMOST all the dwellings clustered on either side of the road and sandwiched between the rice fields on one hand and the Corentyne River on the other, the village of Crabwood Creek may be characterized as a nucleated village. As compared to a dispersed village where each dwelling stands apart and is surrounded by its own plot of land, the nucleated village is conducive to more intimate and face to face relationships among its dwellers. It is perhaps partly for this reason that each individual in Crabwood Creek knows most of the other members of the village. The members of the older generation, in particular, are aware of the early backgrounds and past history of almost every family in the village. In the nucleated village there is also a greater wealth of formal and informal interpersonal social circles. The social circles in which an individual moves habitually include his family of orientation, kinsmen, close friends and relatives. The relationships between families seem to have a generational continuity because in most cases the relations between two persons can be traced back to the relations between their respective parents.

The village is a unit in many respects. That it is a physical unit needs no further elaboration than has been shown elsewhere. Allowing for some inter-village movements it has been noted that the majority of the village dwellers have descended from the original farmers. The continued existence of Crabwood Creek in space and time thus provides us a basis for treating it as a unit of social organization representing organismic solidarity and corporate unity. The people of different social categories living in the village are integrated into its economic, social and ritual patterns by ties of mutual and reciprocal obligations, sanctioned and sustained by traditions or by other generally accepted conventions. The unity of the village is expressed more eloquently in the consciousness of common interest which is symbolized in various forms. It is symbolized spiritually by religious gatherings such as the "Yagya" and "Kali Puja," organized collectively or sometimes individually, attended by one and all. Both the ceremonies are related to Hindu religion, but the conceptual unity of the village is expressed in the form of participation in the ceremonies by Hindus, Moslems and Christians alike. In one of the Yagyas, attended by the investigator, the religious gathering was presided over by a known Brahman priest who preached the orthodox ritualistic beliefs of the Hindu religion, quoting extensively from sacred Hindu scriptures such as the Vedas and the Bhagavad Gita. His sermon was punctuated with frequent warnings to the audience that they should remain on guard against Christian catechists who, according to him, were employing surreptitious methods to dissuade them from their sacred Dharma. While the Brahman priest was sermonizing against the "undesirable" influence of Christian missionaries, an interesting fact remained unnoticed by the audience—the person who was conducting the proceedings of the Yagya, the headmaster of a local school, was himself a Christian.

The other symbols of common interest are local traditions, memories of notable personages and events peculiar to the village itself. According to Redfield, a community is characterized by conventional understandings, the occupation of a territory and the possession of a culture (Redfield 1947). In this sense Crabwood Creek qualifies as a community. One cannot fail to be impressed by the villagers' feelings of pride in their local tradition, in the memories of their past labor and efforts toward the establishment and development of the village, and in retaining what they call the "tradition" and "values" which, in their understanding, are characteristic of their "Motherland"—India. Furthermore it can not remain unnoticed that the people boast that their village girls practice great moral restraint, a traditional Indian value, in face of what is described as a general atmosphere of de-emphasized sexual morality throughout the colony.

In a sense there is little difference between the society of Crabwood Creek and that of other villages having similar environments. In line with other societies the interpersonal relationships in the village are ordered by attaching cultural significance to the factors of kinship, age, and sex. As Linton observes, kinship establishes the relation of the individual with his culturally recognized relatives whereas age and sex establish his relationship with the total society and the particular section of the culture in which he participates (Linton 1960: 870-886). In Crabwood Creek the ordering of interpersonal relationships is guided by these same principles. Yet it must be emphasized that underlying these principles there is a pronounced difference that allows us to speak of the culture of Crabwood Creek in the singular: the complex of customs and beliefs which shapes the lives of the vast majority of the inhabitants—the East Indians—has developed a style which is different from other societies. The Indian culture as translated locally is the ideal culture pattern and norm of life, approved and accepted generally by all the East Indian villagers. In terms of this local version of the Indian culture we find that in Crabwood Creek the factors of kinship, age and sex are being used ideally in determining the status and role of the villagers. The status of every individual in Crabwood Creek is ascribed. If a person does not conform to the Indian traditional norms as locally perceived and if the patterns of behavior accruing from his ascribed status do not fall in line with behavior expected by the local East Indian society, it is construed from this that he is becoming de-Indianized and is succumbing to the Kaffaria[1] ways and manners. It is obvious that the locally developed East Indian cultural tradition and the Indian tradition as it exists in India are not the same. What does make the two cultures similar, however, is the fact that

---

1   Originally a term used by Moslems for a non-Moslem. In Guyana this term is used by East Indians for the Negroes.

both traditions have originated from a common source. The local expression which indicates a concern against the process of de-Indianization thus seems to reflect only the desire of the East Indians to retain Indian cultural emblems, as well as some of the basic contents, as these can serve as symbols of their ethnic identity.

It may be pointed out that the desire of the East Indians to retain their cultural identity does not necessarily imply that changes have not occurred in their traditional socio-cultural system. The arrangement of statuses has changed in response to social and economic conditions prevailing in Guyana. Economic conditions, in particular, have influenced statuses with regard to the system of division of labor in the village. Females now function in ways which once were the exclusive responsibilities of males or young adults. In the weekly village markets one finds more females than males working as salesmen. Men and young adults mostly perform the duties of helpers and assistants. The participation of women in the economic activity has resulted in *de facto* modification of their status in society. Such changes have, however, been accompanied by the persistence of some basic cultural contents of the Indian system such as the continuity of basic status values. As such the *de jure* position of women remains the same.

The discussion of Guyanese East Indian family structure which follows will serve to further elaborate this point.

**Family Structure**

A Hindu family begins with marriage (viva-ha) in the presence of the sacred fire kindled at the wedding. The sacred fire represents the goddess Agni who serves as a presiding deity over the ceremony, witnessing the sacred vows exchanged between the bride and the groom. Once the hands of the bride are accepted in the presence of the deity, the groom, according to "Dharma-sashas,' undertakes to perform all the rites that are intended for the continuity and preservation of the family. Besides performing normal domestic activities and duties he has to offer five great sacrifices—*Brahama-yajna* (sacrifice to the sages of the past), *Pitri-yajna* (sacrifice to the spirits of the ancestors), *deva-yajna* (sacrifice to the gods), *Bhuta-yajna* (sacrifice to alleviate the evil spirits), and *Manushya-yajna* (sacrifice to man by offering him food and hospitality). All these sacrifices are to be offered in the presence of Agni to expiate the sins which a person is presumed to commit in life. No person, according to the Manusimiriti, is believed to attain permanent happiness (Nityam) unless he has offered these sacrifices. In case a person expires without performing the sacrifices, his sons are obligated to offer these "yajnas" in his behalf to insure that his soul attains "nityam" in the life hereafter.[2] It may be noted that three out of the five

---

2 This correlates with the Hindu belief that through one's children one reincarnates himself and thus secures immortality and salvation (Rigveda V 410). In the Mahabharata it is

"yajnas" i.e., "Brahma-yajna," "Pitri-yajna" and "Deva-yajna" prescribe not only the need for the continuance of a Hindu family, but also determine the basic psychology of the Hindu home. The Hindu home becomes a place where not only the living members of the family reside, but also where the forefathers are to be remembered at the time of "Pitri-yajna" and the presence of the past sages and gods is to be recognized through ritual, offerings, and the placing of their visual images for the prosperity, happiness, and continuity of the family. The unbreakable ties with the past ancestry protect the living and provide additional prosperity for the future members of the family. The living members are as such placed in a position analogous to that of trustees of the home which belongs to the "pitris," the ancestors, in the interest of the "putras"—future members. Thus the concept of spiritual continuity becomes the basis of the Hindu family and its traditions. In the final analysis we find not only that the Hindu family is a structural unit performing not only the functions of reproduction, socialization of children, and providing psychological and economic security for its living members (Murdock 1949, Levy and Fallers 1959, Lounsbury 1965), but also that it has the added dimension of the presence of ancestors, sages, and gods who form another segment of the unit and function to insure the spiritual continuity of the family. The Hindu family thus includes a proviso of spiritual continuity that links the preceding generations with the members that are to come into being. As was pointed out earlier the spiritual continuity of the family is secured primarily through the sons. The future life of the parents here and hereafter is thus blessed through the religious and social behavior of their sons in particular, and other members of the family in general. It can therefore be observed that in the Hindu family spiritual sanctions prepare a groundwork for interpersonal relations among the members of the family. Moreover these sanctions give the male offspring an edge over female children. A complex network of rituals and ceremonies involving the widest circle of relatives serves to support and maintain the structure. The East Indian Hindu family of Guyana has not departed from this spiritual basis of its structure brought from India. The whole cycle of rituals and ceremonies regularly performed at weddings in Crabwood Creek subscribe to our understanding that the basis of Indian family structure has remained unchanged. The above statement should not be construed as a digression from the analytical position established for the study. I am not examining cultural continuities and changes in terms of cultural survivals. The main focus of this study is to observe the function of cultural forms, symbols, and some of its basic contents in order to determine the bases of cultural continuities. Various changes have occurred in the family system at the level of younger (third and fourth) generations, and the situation of contact and interaction with the other cultural segments has articulated innovations in the system, but it is significant that these changes

---

mentioned that without an heir, a man's ancestors would be in peril, for there would be no one to offer the gods "pinda" (funeral cake) in their behalf (Mahabharata: Adi Parva 14).

reflect a trend of traditionalizing the innovations. Thus whereas meaningful participation is being made by the East Indians in the emerging society of Guyana, the distinctiveness of the group is kept intact by retaining the cultural forms, symbols and some of the basic contents. We will observe this process in detail by examining the original forms, patterns, and the changing meanings and interpretations of the relationships between the members of the family, and the rituals and ceremonies associated with the organization of the family.

## Marriage

*Selection of the Spouse.* Almost all informants were one in their observations that until the third generation the most acceptable practice was that of arranged marriage. It was the exclusive responsibility of the parents to find life partners for their children. The prospective bride and groom were informed only when everything was arranged between their respective parents. To accept and surrender to the wishes of the parents was considered the ideal behavior for both boys and girls. The third and fourth generations, however, started drifting from the old practice. Many of them asserted for their own free choice which sometimes, despite the resistance of the parents, crossed religious barrier within the ethnic group, if not the racial boundaries between groups. To determine the attitude of the younger generation of East Indians in this area a random sampling of one hundred seventy (95 boys and 75 girls) members of the fourth generation, ranging from the age of fourteen to nineteen was conducted. The results indicated that seventy eight percent (78%) of the boys and ninety two percent (92%) of the girls included in my sample preferred marriage by mutual selection over the old practice of marriage by arrangement. This represents one of the major shifts in attitude among East Indians at the level of the younger generation. The attitudes of the older generation have already been stated above. The figures indicate clearly a swing of the pendulum from marriage by selection to marriage by choice. The figures communicate, with a certain amount of precision, the emerging trend in the younger group. More illuminating than these statistical facts however, are the actual statements made by informants stating the reasons for their preferences, because these statements illustrate the intensity of their feelings on this subject. There is a wide range of reasons given to explain this marriage preference. Those that are most frequently mentioned are enumerated as follows: freedom of choice in selecting life partners would make the marriage more stable; mutual selection leads to mutual compatibility; marriage by mutual selection enables the partners to know each other intimately in terms of their attitudes toward life, personal likes and dislikes, tastes and temperaments, habits and moods. Thus a deep understanding before marriage is considered by this generation a prerequisite to a successful relationship between life partners. In the words of a female informant ($17\frac{1}{2}$ years); "There are many advantages in a marriage of free choice. By doing that the persons concerned will develop an understanding between each other ... and this will lead to a successful marriage because the foundation has (thus) been already laid." For the purpose of analysis it is interesting to note that of all the reasons given in support of mutual choice marriage, the two reasons that stood out most prominently were lack of trust on the part of the younger generation in the judgments of the older generation, and the desire of the younger generation to assume full responsibility for all the decisions regarding their future lives. For instance, one male (16 years) pointed out that "the parents," who belong to the older generation, "cannot understand the interests of the young people" and neither can they "notice the things that we want." He further stated that "When I choose a girl I will not go and choose a girl once she is a girl. I will have to tackle she and I will have to meet she and get to know all about she, then I get marry to she." Another male (16 years) expressed a doubt that if he gives his parents the right to choose his wife, they may for reasons of "money" and "big family," "fix me up with a woman who is old and has about five children. I do not like this." Yet another informant (male $15\frac{1}{2}$ years) remarked "I don't know if they will choose a girl who don't know how to walk with a shoe or a girl who don't know to speak proper English language. But as far as I am concerned I will marry the girl I love, and the girl who could speak proper English." A female informant ($17\frac{1}{2}$ years) expressed her firm belief that "free choice marriage is the best because you would pick up someone suitable for yourself. Your parents do not know you well so they can not select somebody for you." Thus, the desire to assume responsibility and to make decisions regarding one's own future is widely expressed by both males and females of the younger generation. When the investigator prodded further and pointed out that the assumption of such responsibilities carries concomitant risk of losing parental protection and security, the members of both sexes expressed their preparedness to face the situation squarely and one informant (male 17 years) responded that "when you choose a marriage partner by your own free will and anything should happen, you have only yourself to blame for you yourself picked the person for a partner." A female informant ($17\frac{1}{2}$ years) argued that "when the couple marries, they will have equal love for each other. They will not blame any one for their matrimonial troubles because they had made their own way of life."

Thus, whereas the members of the older generation still see merit in the old practice of arranged marriage and support it on the grounds that arranged marriage is part of East Indian tradition and that it also provides more security, the younger generation tends to emphasize that love is the main principle on which the life partnership should rest and the family should be developed. In the absence of love the life between a husband and wife according to the younger generation is absolutely meaningless and vulnerable. Such a life leads to domestic strains, tensions, divorce, and occasionally to suicide. An observation made by a female informant ($17\frac{1}{2}$ years) translates the attitude of the younger generation perhaps much better than any analytic description. She remarked that "to my way of thinking arranged marriage occurred during the past when the people were not so civilized. It is a long time law of far off land.

Marriage without love is just like living as cats and dogs." To this informant a departure from the old East Indian practice means a movement toward civilization.

The practice among the persons of marriageable age today is to select their own life partners and manage to get the word about their choice passed on to their parents. Parents generally tend to agree with the wishes of their sons and daughters because no caste barrier is involved. The consent of the parents is, however, still considered an ideal and most desirable condition in the arrangement of life partnership. The older generation, more often than not, express their desire to exercise their traditional rights and obligations in the selection of spouses for their offspring in order, as they say, to insure the stability of the marriage, but they seldom insist on taking a stand against the wishes of their children unless the other party involved belongs to a different ethnic or racial category. A somewhat reluctant acceptance of the change in attitude is embodied in a phrase expressed to the investigator by a member of the second generation, "Bhaiya (brother) awe (we) helpless, times (have) changed." Despite this change, however, the continuity of the old value is reflected in the methods prevalent in obtaining the parental consent. Of all the permissible methods of consecrating a marriage union in Hindu society (Manusimirith III), the most approved ones are those in which a maiden is "given away as a gift" by the father or her guardian to the groom. A marriage is believed to have remained unconsumated unless certain basic rituals such as *Kanyā-Dāna* (i.e., giving away of the maiden) are performed. Thus, the boy and the girl on finding each other, manipulate the situation in their respective homes in such a way that it appears as if the marriage is being arranged by their parents, and the bride is "given away as a gift." The boy gets the word passed to his parents through a friend or a friendly neighbor. The girl moves the word through a close girl friend, or through a sister-in-law, to her mother who in turn relays the message to the father. When both parents are informed they take initiative at their own level and negotiations start between the elders. Thus it may be seen that the change from parental arrangement of marriage to marriage by mutual choice is a functional adaption of the community to the demands of the Guyanese situation and not to a change in cultural values.

*Rules of Exogamy.* The caste system has ceased to exist in the Guyanese East Indian community at least in the operational sense of the term. Some people know about the caste system and a few can even identify themselves with certain "jāti" groups, but caste related behavior is almost nonexistent. For example in the selection of marriage partners the traditional Indian practice of caste-endogamy is no longer a determining factor.[3] Nevertheless, the rules of exogamy still seem to regulate and control the choice of mates. The rules of Dharmasās-tras that determine the exogamic circle in Hindu marriage are fairly complex.

---

3  For information on the breakdown of the caste system in Guyana see R. T. Smith, and Chandra Jayawardena "Caste and Social Status Among the Indians of Guyana," in Burton M. Schwartz (ed.) Caste in Overseas Indian Communities, San Francisco, Chandler Publishing Company, 1967.

Their persistence in time, if any, would be of importance not in measuring the degrees to which there is conformity to the original structure but in determining whether the cultural pattern, modified by environmental factors, has resulted in the growth of modes of personalities that are similar to those of the original culture or whether they have influenced the development of a new Indian personality in Guyana. The rules of exogamy in Hindu marriage are explained in terms of "gotra" and "sapindā." According to Dharmasāstras and the Grihya-sūtras a person is forbidden to marry within his own "gotra." Thus, all the patrilineally related kins are excluded from the marriage circle. On the mother's side it is ordained that a man shall not marry a woman who is "sapindā" up to the sixth degree in ascending or descending line. In the seventh degree of ascending or descending line the "sapindā" relationship terminates and hence the marriage is permissible. For the term "gotra" there is an equivalent term "Parivār" which is commonly used in Guyana. Persons related to each other through paternal ancestry are said to belong to the same "Parivār." Marriage between the members of the same "Parivār" is strictly forbidden. The word "Parivār" seems to be a corrupt form of "Pravara" which appears frequently in the Hindu Scriptures in the same sense as "gotra." (Mānava-Grihyasutra i, 7, 8; Gautama-Dharmasūtram IV, 2.)[4] In the cult of fire worship among Indo-Aryans, the term, "Pravara" refers to the series of ancestors of the persons who had in former times invoked Agni (god of fire). This religious term which was once used exclusively for cult ancestors had a social bearing and in the course of time the persons linked with the same ancestors came to be perceived as having genetic relationships. Consequently it is laid down that a man shall not marry a woman who can be traced from any of the ancestors as mentioned in his "Pravara" (Prabhu 1958: 156). The word "sapindā" referring to the relatives on the mother's side has not been found in use in Guyana but all informants characterize marriage with one's mother's relatives as an act of incest.

Thus whereas caste observances and the practice of caste endogamy became natural casualties of early demographic imbalance and the working conditions in which the East Indian immigrants were placed (Nath 1950: 208), the conceptual understanding of the exogamic circles still persists and is being translated into practice at this date.

*Wedding Rituals.* It has been seen that the ascribed status and the role of father in the consecration of a marriage union and the practices of "Parivar" and "sapindā" systems in the selection of life partners reflect the continuity of some of the basic Indian values in the Guyanese East Indian community. Why these values have survived and how the group has managed to absorb the major shock administered to its social structure by the loss of the caste system are the obvious questions to which this research is to be addressed. The answers

---

4   For a detailed discussion on the terms "gotra" and "Pravara" see K. Rangachari, "Gotra and Pravara" in Proceedings and Transactions of the Third Oriental Conference, Madras, 1924.

to these questions are to be found in an examination of the changing interpretations of cultural symbols such as the rituals and ceremonies which embody cultural values, and the attitudes of group members at different generational levels. It is obvious that values and attitudes are intangibles. Rituals and ceremonies (a complex of rituals) translate the intangible into the real. As such the participation of a group in a set of rituals reflects its solidarity and symbolizes its commitment to a unified social purpose. This underscores the significance of rituals (both in form and meaning) in measuring the continuities and changes in a socio-cultural system. With this understanding in mind let us examine the social observances and rituals performed on the occasion of marriage in further detail, in order to find out if the forms of the original Hindu rituals and the values symbolized in the rituals are still held by the Hindus in Crabwood Creek.

During the course of field work, the investigator attended several weddings and recorded almost the complete range of rituals and ceremonies performed on each occasion. The individual interpretations of the Pandits were recorded and a cross-checking was done with other Pandits, some of whom lived outside the village, to determine whether there was an element of consistency in their interpretations. The range of interpretation of rituals and ceremonies in terms of their meanings and values was found to be strikingly similar and in most cases completely identical. Despite the fact that almost all the Pandits perform their function only as a part time activity the investigator suspected a possibility that they may have developed shared professional norms, and as such, the identical interpretation of the ritual could be only a function of their shared interests. Inquiries were therefore made at the level of common people in the village to ascertain if they understood the meanings of the Sanskritic terms of the rituals, its forms, and also the values associated with each ritual. Barring some variations of minor importance, the general level of understanding in the older generation (first and second) corresponded quite closely to the interpretations of the Pandits. The Sanskritic terms were more or less a part of the general vocabulary of the older generation. A departure from this trend was noted among members of the younger generation (third and fourth). The members of the third generation were found to be generally aware of the forms of rituals. In case of doubts they seek guidance either from the Pandits or from a person of the older generation, whose knowledge is considered trustworthy. In one wedding attended by the investigator, a "Nawa," (Barber), with whom the family maintained "Jajmani" relationship (Beidelman 1959), was called to make arrangements and help in the performance of all rituals. The presence of "Nawa" and his active participation in the arrangements of the rituals was highly satisfying to the parents of the bride and the groom. They provided all the articles which "Nawa" asked for without asking any questions on the relevance of the articles to the ritual. When the investigator asked the meanings of the rituals from the parents of the bride and the groom, they answered some of the questions and referred the rest to Pandit and to the "Nawa." Thus, when the third generation was compared with the second generation, their knowledge of the underlying values and meanings of rituals was found proportionately reduced but their commitment to the forms of the rituals and their ritual participation remained traditional.

The behavior in this area of the fourth generation was entirely different. In most cases they did not know the forms or the meanings of the rituals at all. The rituals which have their counterparts in the dominant culture are known in this generation by their English equivalents rather than by the original Sanskritic terms. For instance, among the people of this generation the term "engagement" is more popular than its Sanskritic term "chekai." Their participation in the rituals is sometimes so different that it causes embarrassment to elders because it typifies diametrically opposed values.

With this in mind, let us return to the ritual and ceremonies involved in marriage and examine the network of values underlying the rituals and their differential interpretation at the generational levels.

Numerous rituals and ceremonies are involved in a typical Hindu marriage and wedding in Crabwood Creek. To present the local interpretation of all these rituals would be needless and burdensome for my study. I will thus confine myself to an enumeration and very brief description of each ritual. Such description will serve the purpose of presenting the sequence of events leading to the formation of the family unit and will thus provide some insight into the social structure of the family and the network of social obligations and reciprocal relationships that exist in the village society. A few ceremonies which are considered by the members of the community to be vitally important and fundamental will be discussed in more detail in order to exemplify the differential interpretations at the generational levels.

Briefly speaking the rituals involved in a typical marriage and wedding in a Crabwood Creek Hindu family can be classified under three categories: *Dharma-riti*—the rituals that stem from the laws of the sacred Vedas, *Kuli-riti*—the rituals that stem from family traditions, and *Gaon-riti*—the rituals that stem from village traditions. (Specific details of some of these ceremonies will be discussed later.) The following rituals are included under "Dharma-riti."

1. Chekai—This is the engagement ceremony at the groom's house. The Pandit performs "agnihotra" to invoke the blessings of gods and goddesses. Gifts are offered to the groom by the bride's father.

2. Tilak—This ceremony at the groom's house reaffirms the engagement and serves as a general announcement of the proposed marriage. The Pandit declares the relationship irrevocable and instructs the groom to lead a life of abstinence and purity. Invocations are made for the blessings of gods and goddesses and gifts are offered to the groom.

3. Mati-Kore—This ceremony, "digging the dirt," is performed at the homes of both the bride and the groom. The bride's mother and the bride's father's sister accompanied by other ladies walk in the direction of the groom's house. The father's sister picks up dirt from the road and places it in the lap of the bride's mother, while other ladies in the party sing, dance, and make jokes which men are not supposed to watch or hear. The ceremony is enacted in reverse by the groom's mother and his father's sister.

4. "Marua" and "Nuptial Pole"—This is a ceremony to make the "Marua," a booth under which the wedding is performed. The Marua is erected during the same night the Mati-Kore is performed. A green bamboo is planted in the courtyard of the house and a wooden enclosure, "Marua," is made under the bamboo, which is called the Nuptial Pole. The Pandit's presence is necessary. He invokes gods and goddesses when the bamboo is raised and makes an elaborate speech to signify the importance of the Marua and Nuptial Pole.

5. Hardi—This is a ceremony conducted at both houses in which "dai" is rubbed on the bodies of the bride and groom to symbolically purify them. The Pandit makes invocations and token gifts are given by relatives and neighbors.

6. Kumari-Patra and Kumar-Patra—This ceremony is performed at both houses to mark the separation of the bride and groom from their childhood friends. Satya-Narain Katha a meeting where sacred Hindu scriptures are recited by a Pandit, is held for offering thanks to gods and goddesses, and ancestral spirits are invoked for participation and blessings.

7. Baryat—The ceremonial arrival of the groom's party at the house of the bride is called Baryat. The groom is dressed in a modern European style suit covered by a traditional apron, "Jama," and a headgear, "Pat-mauri." The wedding procession is headed by the groom, his father and a Pandit. Near relatives, friends and neighbors form the rest of the procession.

8. Milap—This ceremony at the bride's house takes place to receive the Baryat. The Baryat is received fifteen to twenty yards before it reaches the house by the bride's father, a Pandit and Nawa (barber). The Pandit makes invocations to gods and goddesses, and a cash present is offered by the bride's father to the father of the groom.

9. Janwas—In this ceremony the groom's party is formally welcomed and arrangements are made in the neighborhood of the bride's house for their relaxation. An exchange of promises is made by the bride's father and the groom's father through their respective Pandits signifying their mutual acceptance. Gifts are given to the groom's father and mutual understanding and tolerance in the course of the future relationship between the families is promised.

10. Dwar Pooja—This ceremony is performed at the door step of the bride's house to welcome the groom. A square is made with the Pandits of each party, the bride's father, and the groom sitting across from each other. Invocations are made by each Pandit to Ganesh, Varuna, Lakshmi, Gauri, and Agni, all gods and goddesses of the Hindu religion. Gifts in the form of cash, clothing and utensils are offered to the groom by the bride's father.

11. Parchay—This is the ceremonial worship of the groom inside the bride's home. The bride's mother takes the lead, welcomes the groom, and performs "arti" (worship) of the groom. "Arti" is then repeated by other ladies who are relatives, friends, and other members of the village. Money, tie pins or both are offered as gifts by each lady; all the gifts are recorded by the bride's brother or some other members of the bride's family.

12. Naichu or Nichawar—This is a gift giving ceremony. The bride's

mother's brother brings seven mango leaves which the bride bites, and gives to her mother. The bride sits in the Marua under the Nuptial Pole and her mother sits by her side. This is the occasion when the most gifts are given. All the attendants offer gifts. The mother puts each gift on her head to show it to everyone. The name of the gift giver is announced and a complete record of each gift is maintained so that it may be returned in kind to the giver on a suitable occasion at his house.

13. Vivah—Vivah ceremonies are performed under the Marua. The bride sits in the enclosure under the Nuptial Pole, in front of the Pandit. At this time she is dressed in a costly Indian dress (sari-choli ensemble). The groom's elder brother is called and instructed by the Pandit to undertake the responsibility of taking good care of the bride when she reaches his home as his younger brother's wife. The bride in turn is instructed to obey him as an elder brother and give him all respects without looking into his eyes. The elder brother of the groom indicates acceptance of responsibility by giving the bride some personal gift and a suitcase containing a dress and jewelry. The bride accepts the gift, leaves the Marua, and the groom is then asked to take his place under the Marua. Now the groom worship ceremony (Doolha Pooja) is performed by the bride's father. He washes the groom's feet, offers him "Madhu Parka" (honey, yogurt and churned butter), and Bastra—a piece of cloth upon which to sit comfortably.

14. Kanya Dan—This is a ceremony held to "give the maiden away as a gift." The bride is brought back to the Marua after Doolha Pooja. She sits near her father, facing the groom. The Pandit lights a fire, a dough of flour containing a coin or jewelry is prepared and put into the right hand of the bride, and the father places her right hand in the hand of the groom. The groom accepts her hand, the bride's younger brother pours water on the hands of the bride and groom, and the bride then moves from her father's side to the right side of the groom. The "giving the maiden away" ceremony ends with another major giving of gifts, secondary in importance only to Nichawar. An account of all gifts is again maintained.

15. Lava Havan—In this ceremony Lava (fried rice) is burned in the Havan (fire pit) under the Nuptial Pole. Both parties throw their rice into the Havan, while the Pandit reads "mantras" selected from the scriptures. The Pandit explains this as being symbolic of the bride's release from her previous bonds.

16. Bhanwar—This is a ceremony in which the bride and groom walk around the sacred fire and the Nuptial Pole seven times. It is considered to be an important part of the wedding. The bride takes the lead first and with the groom behind her walks four times around the fire and the Nuptial Pole. Then the groom takes over and leads the bride three times around the fire and the pole. This ceremony is thought to create a sacred tie between the bride and groom with Agni (God of Fire) as a witness.

17. Sat Bachan (Seven vows ceremony)—After Bhanwar, the Pandit recites from scriptures and then helps the bride to obtain seven vows from the groom.

The bride demands that she be consulted whenever: (a) an act of charity is done; (b) a homage is paid to departed relatives; (c) a temple is intended to be constructed; (d) a long journey for business is planned; (e) any duty toward relatives and animal lives is performed. She would also demand to be informed about the profits, loss, income and expenditures in the business transactions. Lastly she demands a promise that she and she alone will be the lawfully wedded wife. When the groom acceeds to all the demands of the bride he asks for her acceptance of one of his demands, i.e., to be faithful to him and act according to the religious rules. The bride gives her acceptance and moves to the left side of the groom. The marriage is now complete. The groom places a ring on the finger of the bride and puts "sendoor" on the parted hair line of her head. A sheet of white cloth is placed over the bride and groom to provide privacy for the "sendoor" pasting ceremony. The Pandit concludes the ceremony with prayers.

*Kuli-riti* are the rituals which stem from family tradition. These traditions have no religious roots but they are widely practiced in India. Since such traditions have been developed in each family, they are considered as unique family traditions which are supposed to be respected by the families of both parties. Among the East Indians in Guyana, each family does not appear to have its own traditions, but some popular and widely practiced family traditions do seem to have migrated from India with the East Indian immigrants. The following traditions were noted in the course of investigation.

1. After the marriage ceremony, the bride retires from the Marua to a room inside the house. The groom is expected to go inside the house to take her away to his home. When he attempts to enter, the sisters and female cousins of the bride block his entry. The groom is generally accompanied by his own brothers or brothers-in-law who try to push their way in. This leads to a small skirmish between the two parties in which the girls hit the groom and his companions with sticks wrapped with flowers. After a short while a truce is made and the groom's party buys its way into the home by making some payment to the bride's sister. Generally G$5.00 is the amount paid.

2. When the groom enters the house he is required to take off his shoes and sit by the side of the bride on a carpet. The bride's younger brother steals the shoes thus placing another hurdle in the way of the groom. A small payment of another sum of money (G$2-$5) is then made to recover the stolen shoes.

3. The bride and groom sit together on the carpet. The sisters-in-law then bring a plate containing bangles. They sit by the side of the couple and toss a bangle in the air. The bride and groom are supposed to catch the bangle while it is in the air. Whoever catches the bangle is supposed to dominate in the household.

*Gaon-riti* are the rituals that stem from village traditions and may be called local traditions. It is not uncommon in India for each village to have its own unique traditions. Indian village traditions have great strength and are supposed to be observed along with the other rituals.

The East Indians in Crabwood Creek seem to have developed two such local traditions in which they have blended Creole cultural traits with those of village India.

1. Badai—When all the rituals inside the bride's house are completed, the bride leaves the groom and shuts herself off in a separate room with some of her best friends and her sisters-in-law. She takes off her traditional Indian dress, the "sari-choli ensemble," and puts on a European style white wedding gown with veil and other accessories. Very great care is taken in making this wedding gown. It is usually made of white lace and a relatively large amount of money is invested to make it look impressive. While the bride is changing her clothing in the other room, the groom takes off his head cover, "Pat-Mauri" and the long colored robe, "Jama," under which he is wearing a well tailored suit. The bride returns and both then walk together hand in hand dressed in European style. Everyone present wishes them good luck. Some coins and rice are thrown over them when they get into the car accompanied by one or two other members of the groom's party.

This mode of the bride's departure from her parental home is diametrically opposed to the practice prevalent in India. In India the bride departs from her home in bright colors (the color white is a sign of mourning). At the time of her departure, she embraces each member of her family and cries loudly to show her grief in leaving her family. If the girl does not cry at this time, she is labeled as a shameless girl who was desirous of leaving her parents' household.

2. Kakan—On the day following the wedding when all the arrangements in the houses of the bride and groom are being brought to an end, the relatives, friends and neighbors assemble in the respective houses to help the household members. The Marua, flowers, rice, and other items used on the wedding day are taken to the riverside and thrown into the river. It is claimed that these articles have been thrown into the sacred river of Hindus, the Ganges. This ceremony is called *Kakan*. The traditional *Kakan* ceremony is then blended with the Creole cultural tradition in which the end of the wedding is marked by a festive celebration. In line with this tradition the *Kakan* assembly turns into a big party. The parents of the bride and groom arrange for goats to be skinned and roasted. A large quantity of rum is also bought for the occasion. The participants drink and eat meat from noon until midnight. Loud gramophone music and dancing accompany the eating and drinking.

It was noted that in the early part of the ceremony when the Marua, flowers, rice and other articles are thrown into the river, the Pandits and the older generation take the most active part. The younger generation does not demonstrate interest in these rituals. However, in the later part of the ceremony when the eating, drinking and dancing is done, it was noted that the indifference of the younger generation turns into active participation. The dances become more and more provocative and overtly suggestive. During this time the older generation recedes into the background.

It will be observed that, in the first category of rituals, i.e., *Dharma-riti*, certain elements are common to almost all the rituals. Firstly, almost every ritual is guided by the Pandit and on many occasions when negotiations are to be conducted by the parties or formal relationships are to be ordered between various categories of relatives of both sides, the Pandits function either as intermediaries or as representatives of their respective parties. The most outstanding function of the Pandit in almost all of the rituals is his invocations of gods and goddesses. No marriage is complete unless it is punctuated by the invocations of gods and goddesses, at the proper time in each ritual. The presence of gods such as Agni, Ganesh, Gauri, and Varuna as witnesses to the ceremonies is considered mandatory. Secondly, most rituals are also marked by the involvement of parents and the participation of other relatives. Each performs his or her role with reference to his or her relationship with the bride and the groom. As a matter of fact, a network or rituals and ceremonies is found to exist which involves the participation of a very wide circle of relatives, friends, and members of the community. Thirdly, the rituals involve frequent presentation of gifts. The frequency of gift exchange is strikingly high. The circle of gift giving is not confined to the parents and near relatives of the bride and groom, but includes distant relatives, friends, and members of the village community. A complete record of all the gifts received during various ceremonies is carefully maintained so that the recipient may reciprocate when some appropriate function or ceremony is held at the house of the giver. Thus a "gift complex" linked with the marriage rituals "involves three elements—giving, receivng, and repaying" (Ishwaran 1966: 139). Informants stated that the prestige of a person is estimated on the basis of the quality and quantity of the gifts that he gives on occasions of marriage in the village. The gift also demonstrates the status of the receiver, because he usually receives the equivalent of what he has given to others on the occasion of their family functions. Thus, in line with the village society in India, the system of gift exchange in Crabwood Creek reflects a complex network of social relationships which involves relatives, friends and members of the village community emphasizing "the need of every body for every body" (Ishwaran 1966: 146).

Most of the rituals in the second category, *Kuli-riti*, are secular and secondary in the order of importance. They involve people of all ages but are more popular among the people of the younger age group.

The rituals that are classified under the third category are blends of Indian and Creole traditions. They are of no major importance in terms of Hindu religion. I will now examine some of these rituals and the participation of different generations in the rituals to observe their respective interpretations, involvement and interest.

It was obvious to me that the rituals placed in the first category were of vital importance to the community. These rituals were reported to have their source of origin in the sacred Hindu scriptures, and were noted to have attracted larger participation than others from those present at all the marriages I attended. They also formed the core of all the marriage activities. On inquiring from the Pandits and other informants, whether some among these rituals had a relatively higher importance than others, the investigator was informed that in as much as all the rituals should be performed in an ideal Hindu marriage, the ceremonies of Chekai or Tilak, Marua, Nuptial Pole, Vivah, Kanya Dan, Lava Havan, and Bhanwar are by far the most important ones and must not be avoided if the marriage is to be considered valid from the point of view of Dharma. The generational behavior during the performance of these ceremonies will therefore be examined in greater detail.

Chekai—Once the marriage has been approved by both families the engagement ceremony, "Chekai", is performed. "Chekai" is the formal initiative taken by the girl's father to propose the "giving away as a gift" of his daughter to the boy. The approach to the boy must be made through his family, particularly through his parents. The "Chekai" ceremony is a form of announcement of the coming marriage which has already been negotiated between the parents through a third party. The participation of the community in the ceremony amounts to a recognition of and acceptance of the proposed relationship. Any social understanding is, however, considered inadequate and revokable unless the engagement is sanctified by proper invocations to gods and goddesses. Thus, on the occasion of the ceremony a Pandit has to be present and a religious ritual "Agnihotra" has to be performed in his presence. During "Agnihotra" invocations are made to "Ganesh," the god of property and love, and "Agni," the god of fire.

The former (Ganesh) is invoked for the establishment of amicable and happy relationships among the members of the families involved and for the prosperity of the individuals intending to marry each other. The latter (Agni) is invoked to be a witness on the occasion in order to sanctify and validate the proposed conjugal relationship. The invocations are made by the Pandit in the presence of the bride's father and the groom who sit on the floor across from each other. The bride's father washes the feet of the groom, puts red ochre on the groom's forehead and places flowers in his hands. The Pandit explains to the groom the meanings symbolized in these actions and asks him to accept the offerings extended by the bride's father. The washing of the feet demonstrates respect and affection, applying red ochre to the forehead signifies the expectation that the groom will henceforth lead a life of purity, and the placement of the flowers signifies a desire for a happy and prosperous life. When this part of the ceremony is completed the bride is "offered as a gift" and the groom indicates his acceptance by saying "swasti" (I accept in the name of God). The ceremony ends with the presentation of a gift by the bride's father to the groom. Informants state that the washing of the groom's feet by the bride's father is an "old time" practice which should be discarded. A member of the younger generation characterized this practice as "uncivilized" and declared that when he would himself be married he would not allow his feet to be washed by the bride's father. Until recently the traditional Indian practice of giving a piece of cloth and some money on such occasions was considered the ideal. Traditionally, this gift was made to reflect appreciation of the groom by the bride's father. Hence it was only a token of acceptance. However, the younger generation has changed the meanings of this gift by emphasizing its material dimensions and by adding to it the element of social prestige. The younger generation now expects a gift of a valuable ring and an amount of money to be given according to the financial standing of the bride's father (G$50-G$700). The prestige of both the parties is evaluated on the basis of the amount of money paid and received on this occasion.

Tilak—The chekai ceremony is followed by a ceremony called "Tilak" which is generally performed one week before the wedding. As stated previously, this ceremony is a form of reaffirmation of the engagement. Near relatives and members of the village community are invited on this occasion to be witnesses to the account of mutual understandings arrived at between the two parties. After the Tilak ceremony, the engagement is taken as final and irrevocable. Both parties make a firm commitment in the presence of the Pandit that they will not break the engagement, and after this breaking of the engagement for any reason is considered to be highly undesirable. The Pandit derives his authority from his assumed knowledge of the scriptures used at this time for the invocations of the deities. He instructs that in order to sanctify the commitment, the parties are not to allow the eating of meat or fish or the drinking of liquor in their respective houses until the wedding is over. During this period the boy is to lead a life of austerity and spend much of his time thinking about his responsibilities as a husband. Gifts are offered to the groom by the bride's father according to his ability to give. This ceremony is taken very seriously by the older generation. The aspects of self purification and mental preparedness have the same degree of strength as other important religious acts. Among the younger generation, however, this period of self purification is observed in the form of a continuous bachelor party in which an excessive amount of liquor is used and sexually oriented jokes are told. Thus, this ceremony, characterized by strong spiritual attitudes in the older generation, has for the younger generation become a purely secular and festive occasion.

Mati-Kore—All the ceremonies mentioned so far are attended exclusively by men. The roles of males and females are very well defined. Women are consulted in all matters but they do not take part in the actual ceremonies. Two days before the wedding date, women take an active part. They assemble in the evening in the houses of the bride and groom and sing marriage songs in Hindi, accompanied by Indian musical instruments such as the "Dholak" (cylindrical drum) and majira. Late at night they start out in the direction of the bride's and groom's houses, respectively. The bride's mother and her father's sister pick up some dirt from the road and bring it inside the bride's house. On their return to the house a green bamboo or Mandap (Nuptial Pole) is planted in the courtyard of the house, and the "Marua" (the booth where the wedding is performed) is prepared around the bamboo. Likewise a Nuptial Pole is planted in the courtyard of the groom's house. In answer to a question about the significance of the bamboo, the Pandit who was present to perform his part in the ceremony explained that "Bamboo has so many knots, so it indicates that the bride and groom ask their gods for the continuity of their family for ages and ages and pray that the family life should grow as the bamboo grows."

The sacred nuptial fire is lighted in both homes under the bamboo by the respective Pandits to insure that all the ceremonies are blessed by Agni, the god of fire. As the bamboo (Nuptial Pole) is raised and the sacred fire (nuptial fire) is lighted, the Pandit delivers a speech quoting extensively from the sacred scriptures to emphasize the importance and the sanctity of the occasion. In all the marriages attended by the investigator it was noted that whereas the members of the older generation, including some from the third generation, paid due respects to the Pandit and demonstrated by their behavior a deep understanding of the solemnity of the occasion, the younger generation paid scant attention to the religious sanctity of the ceremony. On one occasion it was noted that while the Pandit, after lighting the sacred nuptial fire, was delivering his speech, five different groups of young men were playing cards only a few yards from where the Pandit was standing. The card games continued all through the ceremony. Several times when their noise and enjoyment interfered with the speech of the Pandit, he invited their attention and asked them to end their card games at least until the end of the sacred ceremony. His repeated exhortations went unattended by the younger men. It was apparent from the respective behavior of both generations that what was sacred and highly ritualistic for one generation was a purely social and secular affair for the other.

Vivah, Kanya Dan, Lava Havan, and Bhanivar—Details of these ceremonies have been described earlier. It will be observed from the accounts of these ceremonies and rituals that they represent the culminating point of marriage. The gods and goddesses are invoked repeatedly. Every move suggests symbolic forms of spiritual participation. The sacred fire representing Agni which is kept burning in the "Havan" becomes the focal point around which the bride and groom move to take an oath of life partnership. The Pandit continues to recite from the scriptures, and most of the relatives and attendants become witnesses to the sacred tie of marriage, which once established, is not allowed to be broken. Hindu marriage is thus a sacrament, and during the performance of these rituals a climatic level of spiritual performance is attained. The older generation witnesses these rituals and ceremonies as outstanding sacred events which, according to the Pandits, tend to solidify the social relationships between relatives, friends, and members of the community. The behavior of the younger generation at such spiritually oriented events again exemplifies an entirely different attitude. At all the marriages I attended it was noted that most of the time the members of the younger generation stay away from the Marua and sacred fire. Generally they group together in a separate house across the street, where they drink rum, usually to excess, while the ceremonies are being performed. Marriage is an event of excitement to the members of the younger generation, not because an important religious function is being performed, but because it provides them an opportunity to drink together with their age mates. Indian film music is played and amplified on loud speakers, and young men demonstrate their skill in dancing a blend of Indian and Calypso type dances. Often they move toward the house of the bride where they assemble in the middle of the road and through suggestive dances attract the attention of girls participating in the ceremony. The girls do not actively participate in such dances, but give encouragement to the boys by indirect participation through smiles and gestures. This behavior by the younger generation causes annoyance and embarassment to the older generation. The latter wish to retain their traditional ritualistic form which symbolizes the sanctity of the occasion, but the younger generation demonstrates a ritual participation that is more in line with that of the Creole culture.

The departure of the bride from her home to the groom's house (Badai) marks an almost complete break from traditional culture. As stated previously, the bride changes her traditional Indian sari-choli ensemble to a European style white wedding gown with veil and wears western style makeup. The groom removes his head cover "Pat-Mauri" and outer gown "Jama" and is now seen in his European style suit. The bride and groom, holding hands and smiling, depart with members of the groom's party for the groom's house. In India this moment is loaded with emotions. At the time of departure from her parent's home, the bride hugs and embraces each member of her family and cries loudly to express her grief on the event of separation. The white color is considered to be ominous, and the dress worn on this occasion is made of bright red material embroidered with gold and silver.

In summary, it can be seen from the above analysis that on the occasions of the ceremonies which have been described the behavior of the younger generation here stands in sharp contrast with traditional Indian culture, and reflects a significant change in cultural values.

## Caste System

In India, society in each district is comprised of a small-scale hierarchy of "jati" and each jati has a self-contained system of its own. Nationally, thousands of these jati are ranked in a hierarchy of four Varna categories: Brahamin, Kshatriya, Vaisya, and Sudra.[5] Since the ranking of jati is supposed to be immutable, and membership in a jati is acquired at birth and remains non-transferable, this system has been treated by social scientists as an ideal framework for the analysis of the social organization of Indian communities. This explains why the phenomenon of the caste system has been examined so extensively in studies of the social system of communities in India, as well as in studies of Indian settlements overseas.

---

5   G. S. Ghurye states that there are an estimated 2000 jati in each linguistic area. (Ghurye, G. S., *Caste and Race in India*, London, 1932, p. 27).

If the caste system is employed as a tool for the analysis of the social organization of East Indians in Crabwood Creek in the same way as it has been employed for the study of Indian societies, the results will hardly be meaningful. There is scarcely any doubt that the caste system as it exists among East Indians in Crabwood Creek cannot be characterized as a defined system of the "structured relationship" (Kuper 1960: 244) of the group. Researches oriented toward the delineation of the position of the caste system in various areas of the Caribbean have eventually arrived at the conclusion that despite the fact that named caste populations do still exist (Clarke 1967: 172; Schwartz 1967: 126, 143) and the Brahamin priesthood continues to have caste connotation (Clarke 1967: 168; R. T. Smith and C. Jayawardena 1967: 57) the operation of the caste system in the sense that it is practiced in India is non-existent (Clarke 1967: 168; Schwartz 1967: 136, 143). Implicit in the system of the caste structure of Hindu society are certain specific characteristics such as the notion of ascribed status by the incidence of birth; a hierarchy based on Varna membership; occupational division of the society; the concepts of ritual purity, caste endogamy, village exogamy; the practice of commensality; and the patterns of hypergamous and hypogamous marriages. None of these characteristics seem to exist in Crabwood Creek. In a purely structural definition the caste system is defined as "a hierarchy of endogamous divisions in which membership is hereditary and permanent" (Berreman 1967: 120). Ethnographic data collected on the subject in Crabwood Creek fails to support even this structural definition. However, at this point in our discussion it may not be irrelevant to examine whether the caste system should be perceived as a purely social-structural phenomenon of Indian society, or whether it can also be treated as a general institution which serves to provide an ideology to the group and hence functions as an organizing principle of the community. For a broader understanding it would appear that to completely rule out the existence of the caste system on the basis of the absence of certain of its specific characteristics would amount to an abbreviation of the actual concept of the system. It is suggested that a comprehensive view of the caste system should include the treatment of the system at two different levels: a. structural and, b. ideational.

At the structural level the caste system can be viewed as providing a framework for understanding the scheme of social ranking and stratification in Indian society. It may also serve to explain the wider connection between caste and occupation existent in Indian society.

However, when we view caste from the ideational level we are able to see that the structural classification of Indian society alone does not constitute the caste system. The scheme of social ranking and stratification as it exists under the caste system is based on certain ideational attributes of each rank (jati) that are expressed in Hindu scriptures and are further reinforced through the tradition of ritual purity, occupational specializations, and separate modes of behavior. The structure of Hindu society without this ideational basis is not perceived as the caste system by Hindus.

Thus the caste system is not only a scheme of social stratification but is also an idealogy. A comprehensive view of the caste system should encapsulate a treatment of the system at both levels.

With this concept of the caste system in mind, let us examine the East Indian society in Crabwood Creek. As stated earlier, the caste system can no longer be explained as a "defined system of the structured relationship" with reference to the East Indian group in the village of Crabwood Creek. The social, political, economic and juridic relations among the members of the East Indian community are not based on caste lines. This is true for the village as well as for the whole country of Guyana where early demographic imbalance and working conditions on plantations made the survival of the caste based structure of East Indian society impossible. In the face of adverse circumstances the East Indians acquired new idioms of social relationship in which caste observances and practices became less important. The caste based rules of occupational hierarchy, ritual purity, endogamy, and commensality, etc. were replaced by practices guided by the expediencies of the new situation. In effect the entire East Indian community became more or less a single caste, and members of other racial categories such as Portuguese, Chinese, Negroes, and Amerindians became other castes with whom differential social relationships were established. Data collected on this subject at the generational level in the village of Crabwood Creek demonstrate the following patterns.

All members of the older generation interviewed by the investigator knew the names of their own jati and could place themselves in the appropriate Varna category. They were also aware of the jati and the Varna category of their spouses. On a sampling covering eighty couples, sixty-six marriages (82.5 per cent) were intercaste marriages. Thus in Crabwood Creek caste can hardly be called an endogamous unit. Since the choice of life partners in most cases was dictated by the factor of the availability of males and females, the patterns of hypergamy and hypogamy could not be determined. Except for the Brahmin priests who enjoy a unique status as a result of their role in certain ritual performances, there appears to be no correlation between caste origins and status distribution.

Unlike the practice in India there is no organized system of jati group separation and interdependence except in the case of the Nawa (barber) who performs certain assigned roles and maintains a sort of "jajmani" relationship with all members of the community (Beidelman 1959).

It is difficult to delineate the actual status of Brahmin priests in the society. They acquire a special position on the occasion of marriage and Harikatha. Some informants also report that Brahmin priests are occasionally asked to name a child and to determine favorable dates for marriage. However, such is not the popular practice. The Brahmin priests are an organized group. They have formed an organization at the national level named the Guyana Pandit Council. However, except for a very few Pandits who live in Georgetown, all perform their priestly functions on a part time basis. Brahmin priests are looked upon with respect. This respect and their high status stem from the fact that their presence is necessary for sanctifying marriage rituals, for the performance of "puja" (ritual worship), and for the narration of mythological stories on the occasion of Harikatha. It is significant to note that all of these functions are involved with matters of communal importance and symbolize community spirit. Brahmin priests are accepted as men of special status by the younger generation as well, since it is believed that the Brahmins know about Hindu Dharma and can "enlighten" them on Indian cultural traditions.

It has been stated earlier that caste in Crabwood Creek is not an endogamous unit, however, the circle of endogamy becomes sharply defined when the question of inter-racial marriage is raised. All informants disapproved of inter-racial marriage. Most of them preferred marriage within the Hindu religion regardless of caste.

Members of the younger generation showed complete indifference toward the caste system. Although most of them could name their caste, they fail to place themselves in the proper Varna category. Whenever questions were asked on this subject they invariably stated that "caste na mean nothing to we." On further questioning they emphasized that all Indians are "brothers." Thus it would appear that status equality exists regardless of caste origin and religious affiliation. In a sense, the members of this generation perceive the entire community of East Indians as a single caste.

Thus it will be noted that caste awareness has changed from caste identification at the older generational level to caste indifference at the level of the younger generation. As a result of this change, caste has been reinterpreted by the younger generation and caste endogamy has come to mean marriage within the East Indian group. The investigator observed two marriages in which the bride and the groom belonged to different religions (Hindu and Muslim) but to the same racial stock. No one expressed surprise or concern on either marriage, although it appeared quite surprising to the investigator, who knew that an interreligious marriage in India would normally cause a riot between the two religious communities. An interesting observation made by a young high school teacher in the course of an interview reflects eloquently the views of the younger generation on the caste system: he remarked that, "it is not necessary that a man who acts as Pandit in Yagya must be a Brahmin." On another occasion when two groups of East Indians in the village were about ready to fight with each other, the teacher intervened and admonished the ring leaders of each group by saying that they were behaving like members of "neech jati" (low caste). Both expressions reflect a shift in the meaning of the caste system. Instead of treating the caste system as the basis of social stratification the younger generation looks upon it as a system of measuring personal attributes.

Thus even though the caste system has ceased to be a basis of social stratification among East Indians and the structural characteristics of caste carry little importance, the ideational attributes of caste have continued to be retained through the reinterpretation of caste by the younger generation.

CHAPTER EIGHT

# Religious Institutions: Concepts and Definitions

AN UNDERSTANDING of the religious system of the East Indians in Crabwood Creek is indispensible for the comprehension of my research problem i.e., the nature of cultural continuities and changes, in which the functions of cultural forms, symbols, and basic contents that provide elements of distinctiveness to the group are being examined. All religious systems tend to share three main characteristics. Theoretically, a religion represents a system of beliefs; practically, it forms a system of worship; and sociologically it establishes a system of social relationship (Joachim Wach quoted by Milton Yinger 1957: 12). If we accept these characteristics of a religious system it follows that concepts and symbols, religious dogmas and rituals, and religious institutions and sacred places tend to unify the social systems of which they are a part. All these elements lend to the social system a mystical value, which promotes unity of purpose, group solidarity, and cultural integration. The religiosity of the East Indians in Guyana has been an outstanding characteristic for well over a century and is no less distinctive of the culture today.

The East Indians in Crabwood Creek are divided into three religious groups: Hindus, Muslims, and Christians. The Hindus form 81 per cent of the population, the Muslims 13 per cent, and the Christians 6 per cent.

## Hindus

The Hindus are divided into two groups, Sanatan Dharam (Orthodox) and Arya Samaj (Reformists). An overwhelming number of Hindus are Sanatan in their beliefs. The literal meaning of Sanatan Dharma is "eternal religion." This term in its historical context is said to indicate the "eternal" principles of religion and conduct that are considered to be fundamental truths of Hinduism. Thus Sanatani Hindus follow the orthodox prescriptions, dogmas, rituals, customs, values, and all other beliefs and rites that constitute a fundamentalist's view of Hindu religion. "A Hindu is a man who generally follows the rules of conduct and ceremonial... laid down for him, particularly regarding food and marriage and the adoration of the gods" (Lyall 1889: 14). The Sanatan Dharma emphasizes the continuity of the faith in its ritualistic-puristic form. The Sanatan Dharma is organized at the national level in the form of B. G. Sanatan Dharma Maha Sabha. This organization has a strong following among Hindus in all parts of the colony. According to the national secretary of the

Maha Sabha the organization was founded in 1934, however, it was incorporated under a government ordinance in 1954. In any event its origin and particularly its organizational activity are fairly recent. At present the Maha Sabha is the most active organization among Guyanese Hindus. Its activities cover programs ranging from purely religious propagation and the revival of old and orthodox Hindu traditions to the arrangement of cultural activities and the formation of Hindu public opinion on political issues. The Sanatan Dharma Maha Sabha carries on its activities through the media of a weekly newspaper, the publication of a series of pamphlets on religious topics, and a regular program of religious broadcasts on Guyana Radio. The local branches of Maha Sabha function as agencies of the central organization and serve as important links between local Hindu communities and the organization operating at the national level. The local branch in Crabwood Creek initiates and organizes its own program, in line, of course, with the program of the national Maha Sabha, for the spiritual and cultural needs of the Hindus in the village.

The second group of Hindus, Arya Samaj, have a smaller following. The Arya Samaj movement was started in India in the late nineteenth century (1875) by Dayanand Saraswati and is characterized as a reform movement in the Hindu religion. The main thrust of the movement was directed toward social and religious reforms in Hindu society which, according to the founder of Arya Samaj, was too much preoccupied "with superfluous rituals, sponsored by Brahmin priests" (Heimsath 1964: 121). In terms of the depth of its influence Arya Samaj is considered to have been the most popularly accepted single movement in India during the late nineteenth and early twentieth century. According to an informant who practices Arya Samaj this movement was first introduced in Guyana by Mehta Jayamuni in 1920 followed by the brief visit of another Arya Samaj preacher, Ayudhya Pershad, in 1928. The real impact of the movement was, however, felt later when Professor Bhaskarananda visited Guyana in 1934 and spent ten years in the colony preaching the Arya Samaj concept of Hinduism. During his stay Professor Bhaskarananda founded Guyana Oriental College which became the center of this movement in the colony. Since that time the movement has gained in popularity and followers of Arya Samaj are now found in various parts of Guyana. Thirteen Arya Samaj families were reported living in Crabwood Creek at the time of this study.

The major theological differences between Sanatan Dharma and Arya Samaj as reported by informants, are as follows:

1. Arya Samaj is opposed to Murti Puja (idol worship) which is an outstanding feature of Sanatan Dharma.

2. Arya Samaj emphasizes the unity of god. Brahma, Vishnu, and Shiva are thought to be different attributes of one and the same god. All other deities are considered to be merely humans, who have attained higher levels of spiritualism. One Arya Samaj informant expressed the view that "Devatas and Devis are essentially humans and serve as gods and goddesses to a Hindu in the observance of religion. They are not divine incarnations." This belief stands

in contrast to the Sanatan Dharma's concept of a Hindu pantheon of deities in which each deity is accepted as a god incarnate.

3. According to Arya Samaj a person achieves communion with god through yoga and meditation. The Sanatan Dharma worship their gods in the form of idols (Murti).

4. Sanatan Dharma believes in the caste system and in the ascription of statuses by birth. The Arya Samaj opposes the caste system and believes that a person is not born in any Varna; he is instead identified as a member of a Varna (Brahamin, Kshatriya, Vaishya, or Sudra) according to the kind of life he leads. Thus, in Arya Samaj, caste status is acquired through Karma, the deeds of man. In the words of an Arya Samaj informant, "Vishvamitra was a Kshatriya but became Brahmin by his virtuous conduct, and Ravan was a Brahmin but turned 'Rakshash' (polluted) by his misdeeds."

5. Whereas Arya Samaj believes in obedience and service to parents during their lifetime, Sanatan Dharma emphasizes the continuity of this relationship between parents and their offspring in life after death.

It will be observed from the above facts that Arya Samaj is not a departure from Hinduism. It represents a mode of syncretic adjustment of Hinduism with the nineteenth and twentieth century intellectual and social trends generated in Indian society by its exposure to Islam and Christianity. By believing the Vedas to be timeless, revealed truth, divine in origin (Heimsath 1964: 122), and by proclaiming that the Vedas are the source of all knowledge, Arya Samaj gives the followers of Hinduism a sense of pride in their religion and "allows the educated (Hindu) man to regard himself as still a Hindu, while freeing himself from the burden of much of the superstition, against the absurdity and depravity of which his education has led him to rebel. He welcomes this new version of Hinduism with a sigh of relief" (Holland 1907: 535).

Both the Sanatan Dharma and Arya Samaj versions of Hinduism are practiced in Crabwood Creek apparently without any strained relationships between their respective followers. As a matter of fact a kind of symbiotic relationship has been worked out between the two groups. Those who have a more western orientation, and who tend to present their religion in a rational way to non-Hindus—and there are more of this kind in the younger generation—make use of the Arya Samaj view. The more tradition oriented find more meaning in the continuity of traditional Hinduism by following Sanatan Dharma.

## Muslims

As stated earlier thirteen per cent of the East Indians in Crabwood Creek are Muslims. All of them belong to the Sunni sect of Islam. The Muslim mosque located on Grant Number 1780 serves as the focal point of their religious activities. Daily attendance at the mosque is very poor but the weekly congregation on Friday is well attended.

Attached to the mosque is a Madrassa where arrangements have been made to teach Arabic and the elementary principles of Islam to the children. A unique religious practice has evolved as a local tradition which seems to function as a strong element of social integration among the Muslim East Indians of the village. This practice is known as "Quran Parhey" which means literally, the "recitation of Quran." In terms of this locally developed tradition, Muslim families of the village are required to participate in the recitation of the Quran on all occasions of social importance or individual concerns. Events such as birth, marriage, death, illness, promotion in service, construction of house, new business enterprise, etc. are treated as matters of common interest at which times representatives from each family assemble at the house of the individual concerned and recite from Quran. Thus, the "Quran Parhey" tradition involves relationships based on reciprocity and mutual obligation. Both individual and collective grievances against a family or a member of a family are expressed in the form of non-participation in the "Quran Parhey" ceremony. A large attendance on such occasions is discussed with a sense of pride and is perceived as an indicator of one's acceptance, popularity, and prestige in his communal group. Frequent visitations on the occasions of the "Quran Parhey" ceremony also function as an effective form of communication among members of the group. Through participation and non-participation the "Quran Parhey" ceremony also becomes an effective method of social sanction and control. As such it contributes to the solidarity of the group and creates a feeling of oneness.

## Christians

Six per cent of the East Indians in Crabwood Creek are Christians. Most of them are Protestants affiliated with the Canadian Mission Church. Even though few in number, their numerical strength is strategic to the understanding of my research problem. Guyanese colonial history is replete with facts on how the plantation management and the colonial administration exercised direct and indirect pressures to convert East Indians to the Christian faith. Not only were Christian missionary activities patronized by the colonial administration but various government positions and civil services were reserved for Christians only. Until very recently no person could become a teacher in Guyana unless he had accepted Christianity. Moreover, traditional Hindu and Muslim marriages were considered to be illegal until 1946. To legalize a marriage East Indians had to marry in a Christian church. By implication, if the marriages of the East Indians were conducted according to their own customs, their offspring were not considered legitimate and hence were denied the right of inheritance to property (Commins 1892: 33). It is significant that despite the increased chances of self-advancement available through a change of their religion, the East Indians took the option of staying under the burden of stifling restrictions rather than leaving their faith.

The Public School System in Guyana has been introduced very recently (1956). Prior to this time most of the educational institutions were run by Christian missionaries who "taught catechism, the commandments and the New Testament" (Commins 1892: 28). Informants state that many parents did not send their children to these schools because they feared that their children would be swayed away from their own faith, traditional values, and culture.

It has been demonstrated that East Indians in Crabwood Creek are divided into three major religions: Hindu, Muslim, and Christian, in order of their numerical strength. It is obvious that each of these three religions represents a different system of beliefs and consequently enforces different standards of behavior. If the social interaction between these religious groups were to be observed in India where the followers of each religion belong to the same ethnic stock, an atmosphere of extreme hostility, intolerance and mutual doubt would be reflected. India has been frequented by numberless major and minor communal riots involving all three religious groups during the first half of this century. However, the group of East Indians in Crabwood Creek with almost the same ratio of religious populations as exists in India represents a different situation.

In Crabwood Creek, East Indian religious membership is spread over the three denominations but the people are bound together by a common stock of core values and share a strong sense of peoplehood. By way of illustration a Christian (Anglican) informant, who had been converted to Christianity at the age of twelve and married a Hindu woman at the age of twenty stated that no one had ever objected to his marriage. He further added, "I myself never felt odd, because it was the normal course." Another East Indian informant (Methodist) who is married to a Muslim woman did not see any problem in his interreligious marriage because his wife is "after all an East Indian." A Muslim informant consulted both the Brahmin priests and the Muslim priest in setting the dates for the marriages of his two daughters. At the time of this study he was looking for a husband for his third daughter and observed that if the boy was a good match for his daughter it would not matter whether he was a Muslim, Hindu or Christian. However, he would not accept a proposal from a Negro. When asked why he would not accept a Negro as a son-in-law the informant replied, "If God me created in one racial group of Indians, me na right to change a group by marry me daughter with some body of other race...Me na allow me daughter to marry Negro to destroy me race anyhow." These facts support my premise that the East Indians should be examined as a part of the life that is going on in Guyana and with a cognizance of the culture posture that it is devloping as one of the major components in the merging society of this colony.

The statements by informants subscribe to our understanding that the strong sense of ethnic identity among East Indians in Crabwood Creek has transcended religious differences. A sense of group cohesion has developed, based upon an aggregate of values which have been developed locally on the basis of the group's cultural residue and labeled as Indian tradition.

## The Role of Religion Among East Indians in Developing an Aggregate of Values

Religions have played a major role in the development of an aggregate of values among East Indians in Crabwood Creek. The status of the father in the East Indian family has been reinforced by the religious expressions of his role. Even though we find that the older interfamily patterns of economic cooperation have been disturbed in the process of adjustment with the local Guyanese situation, the father continues to be the source of authority and discipline in the family unit. He determines the basic interaction pattern among members of the family, between family members and the neighborhood, and also their interaction with the village at large. As a person charged by his religion with the responsibility of carrying on family tradition, and in his position as intermediary between the Putras and Pitris, it is the father's role to determine the social and spiritual activities in which his wife and children will participate. His status in the family is thus determined through religious beliefs and ritual participations.

The position of the female in the society and the basic concept of the purity and chastity of the female are well established and constantly reinforced through religious ceremonies and ritual participations. In public the sexes are normally segregated. Traditional Indian religious beliefs have sanctioned the segregation of males and females on ritualistic and social occasions and this practice has been continued in Guyana.

The basic status values are held to be good because religion has sanctioned them. The older men in the village sustain their higher position in the social hierarchy because religion has fortified their status. By holding the oldest male member responsible for the spiritual welfare of the family and by accepting a man's spiritual enlightenment and renunciation of worldly pleasures as indicators of prestige, the society ensures that the elders continue to exercise judicial and authoritarian functions in the village society.

The ethical standards of the East Indian society in Crabwood Creek stem from the traditional Indian ethical system. Non-violence, spiritualism, sacrifice, self-discipline, modesty, charity, contentment, constant introspection, purity of mind, thrift, containment of worldly desire, right means for right goals, and dedicated service to other members of the community are the ideals of Indian ethics (Proceedings of All India Colloquium 1967: 60-110). These ideals are constantly preached in the Yagya and Harikatha which are frequently organized in the village. The frequency of the Yagya is reported to have increased during the past decade, a period known for racial strife and tension in Guyana. Similar ethical principles are preached during Friday congregations in the Muslim mosque and at Sunday services in the Christian church. These ethical standards, conveyed through constant reminders on religious and ritualistic occasions, have now become a part of the conscience of the group. The East Indians of the village tend to use them as identifying features of the group. To non-Indians some of these ethical standards seem so incompatible with their own western oriented value system that they attribute them to the "backwardness" of East Indians. Skinner in his study on ethnic interaction in a Guyanese rural community (1955: 120) has noted that "many Negroes feel that the East Indians have accepted lower standards of living." The ethical standards of thrift, contentment, and containment of worldly desires are thus interpreted as the acceptance of a lower standard of living, and as a trait of penuriousness among East Indians. Nevertheless the East Indians describe these ethical standards with an enormous sense of pride and perceive them as a mark of distinctiveness.

**Religious Festivals**

Religious festivals are occasions in which group solidarity is manifested in an intensified form. The main religious festivals observed in the village are: Basant Panchami (Commencement of the Spring), Shewratri, Phagova, Deepavali, Ram Nomi, Janam Ashtami (Birth of Lord Krishna), Katik Ashnan, Eid, Bara Wafat (Birthday of Prophet Mohammed), and Christmas. All these festivals are marked by the participation of one and all, regardless of religious affiliation. This common participation is, however, restricted only to the group of East Indians. Even on occasions such as Christmas when members of different racial stock have valid grounds for common participation, the celebrations of the event are confined within the boundaries defined by ethnic affiliation.

It was reported to me that very recently an active female member of the Indian Cultural Council has added one more festival to the group mentioned above. The festival, Raksha Bandhan, originated in India and is noted for its popularity and unique emotional characteristics. On the day of Raksha Bandhan a girl can establish a sibling relationship with any boy by tying a band around his wrist. Indian sources yield evidence that once the band is allowed to be tied, and the relationship is accepted by the boy, the two enter into a sibling relationship which involves a network of social obligations and responsibilities on the part of both the members. Historical sources provide evidence that such relationships have been established in the past even to the extent of cutting across the religious boundaries between Hindus and Muslims. The popularity of this festival among East Indians in Guyana is a public expression of the strong sense of peoplehood being institutionalized through a ritual borrowed from Indian tradition.

CHAPTER NINE

# Summary and Conclusions

THE OBJECTIVES of the present study were presented in the opening chapter. It has been stated that the primary purpose of the study is an examination of the process of cultural continuities and change among East Indians in Guyana. The group of East Indians has been viewed as one of the major components in the emerging society of Guyana, and the culture of the group has been observed in the Guyanese setting in which it is today enmeshed. The method of analysis used in this study is based on a firm understanding that the study of East Indian group life within a set of controlled social environments which both inhibit contacts with the parent culture and generate constant interaction with other cultural segments of the society, is likely to yield certain results that would allow us to re-examine the notion of cultural continuities and changes and as such would add some new dimensions to the study of the cultural process.

A survey of the published and unpublished literature on Caribbean studies revealed that the area has been subjected to various research approaches by Caribbean scholars. Caribbean society is a diversified society. It is known for its multi-ethnic, multi-racial composition, and for the characteristic feature of its complexity which has developed as a result of such diversification. A sociological analysis of a diversified society obviously raises the problem of an adequate theory of group relations. Some of the theoretical developments that have emerged from anthropological studies in the Caribbean have been discussed in Chapter II, and attest to my understanding that, as stated earlier, in a very real sense Caribbean studies today appear to be a microcosmic representation of the multiplicity of theoretical approaches and frameworks that together form the anthropological macrocosm. It has been noted, however, that the various theoretical approaches employed in the studies of Caribbean societies are, of late, beginning to synthesize around two theoretical models: the plural society model, and the consensual or unitary model. The plural model depicts society as comprised of more than one cultural section, each having a separate and distinct institutional system with no functional integration of the sections at the total societal level, whereas the unitary model defines society as a system of action in which a set of shared values, shared ideas about means and ends, and a general will are necessary prerequisites for the existence and maintenance of the society. Both models have their relative importance since it is obvious that the study of a diversified society poses numerous problems and raises various types of questions which no single model can possibly answer to the entire satisfaction of an investigator. Studies based on the application of both models have shown that each model affords answers to a different set of questions. Hence, it is asserted that the relevance of the models depends essentially upon the nature of inquiry. It has been suggested in this study that there exists a possibility of combining these so-called competing and mutually exclusive models and of using them as complementary approaches applied simultaneously. By using the two models as complementary approaches it appeared possible to gain an understanding of both the existing institutional arrangements of the group and the cultural posture that is developing in the emerging society as a result of interaction with other cultural segments. With this framework in mind a selected group of East Indians in Crabwood Creek was analyzed, focusing on a problem which, to the understanding of the investigator, has not yet been given the amount of attention that it deserves. Instead of examining Guyana as one large society composed of numerous individuals and groups, the research was directed only to the study of the nature of group life itself within one segment of the large multi-ethnic, multi-racial Guyanese society. For methodological reasons the selection of a microcosm of the East Indian group in the village of Crabwood Creek was made.

It is obvious that in the larger society of Guyana where constitutional documents provide a single guide line for the entire society and where political rights are distributed on a single criterion, regardless of ethnic and racial delimitations within the society, the nature of a group structure would, for the most part, be legally invisible. It may be noted, however, that the absence of legal visibility does not preclude the existence of the group in a sociological sense. In other words, the social and cultural outlines, as developed and perceived by the members of each group, although formally unrecognized, continue to remain in a sociological sense distinctly real. If these socio-cultural outlines and contours are not recognized, our judgments are likely to be clouded and based upon a collection of vague perceptions, "the stereotyped and usually ill-informed views (that) each ethnic group" tends to hold of other groups (Morris 1968: 178).

Thus even when we agree that the search for an adequate model is a matter of importance to an investigator if he is to draw comparative generalizations from similar societies, it is asserted that the present mode of inquiry, being substantially different, gives the investigator freedom to refrain from making full commitment to any particular model. Morris puts the same thing rather differently when he observes that "the collective view which people have of their own society is made not for comparision but to explain their situation satisfactorily to themselves" in the larger context of the society as a whole (1968: 170). As such, the nature of this inquiry permits the investigator to make a selective use of different models so that we may succeed not only in grasping the existing institutional arrangement within the group but also in recognizing the mode of articulation of its institutions in order to understand the dynamics of the group's relationship within the larger society.

Pursuing this line of analysis, I have called attention to the nature of the group of East Indians in Crabwood Creek and have observed for this group the functions of its cultural forms, symbols, and some of the basic contents that have been retained. I have explained in a preceding chapter the historical process through which the racial groups in Guyana have emerged as exclusive units of cooperation. To the East Indians their own cultural forms, symbols, and some of the basic contents such as ethical standards and spiritual values have provided a good foundation for such cooperative endeavors. As a consequence of sharing a number of social and cultural traits, they have developed a strong sense of what we can call "Being an Indian." These retained cultural forms in this situation have assumed new importance and relevancy to the group because they provide a valid basis of ethnic identity. These forms, symbols, and other cultural contents provide the group with a sense of "special ancestral identification" and they perceive themselves as an ethnic group with a common future orientation. This sense of ethnic belonging is often expressed by the use of a local term "Apan Jaat" (our nation) which is used to refer to all East Indians in Guyana regardless of their religious affiliations. The frequency of the use of the term "Apan Jaat" increases or decreases in proportion to the needs of the group. For example, when elections are held, and the desire of the group is expressed in order to validate their claim to political privileges in the society, the term "Apan Jaat" is used in the form of a frequently repeated political slogan to unify the group around its political interests. In every day life the same term is used to identify East Indians as opposed to the other ethnic or racial groups in the colony. These usages of the term testify that East Indians have a conceptualized understanding of themselves as a group and also that they share a "sense of peoplehood."

It has been my contention that the notion of cultural continuities and changes among the East Indians in Guyana should be examined with reference to two major contexts: a) continuities and changes among East Indians as an ethnic group in relation to other groups; b) continuities and changes among East Indians at the generation level. The two contexts have a dialectical relationship with each other. Cultural continuities usually become the first victims of fragmentation as a result of increasing contact with other cultural segments at the descending generational levels, and yet the group as a whole needs these same cultural resources that it fragments for the maintenance of its distinctiveness and identity in the society.

This poses a difficult problem for research and analysis, but it is interesting to note that the resolution of this problem also provides an insight into the processes of culture. Before I proceed further in my discussion, it is necessary to define certain terms which are to be used in this analysis, particularly when these terms are being employed in general usage and also in technical usage in anthropological literature to convey different meanings in different situations.

Ethnic group—Ethnic group is a category of individuals bound together by an emotional bond in a manner which develops a sort of "characterological configuration" and a shared feeling of peoplehood, creating for its members a sociological condition in which they find a responsive agglomeration of their own kind which gives them a sense of identity.

Ethnicity—Ethnicity means a shared sense of ancestral identification among the members of an ethnic group by which they tend to make commitment with the ritualistic-puristic tradition of the group. The term implies commitment to the total cultural tradition of the past.

Ethnic identity—This term refers to a general "sense of peoplehood" among the members of an ethnic group blended with a common future orientation. The sense of peoplehood is based partly on common cultural ties, but the identification with the traditional culture tends to be more symbolic than real.

Let us now proceed with the examination of the cultural process among the East Indians in Crabwood Creek. It has been observed that due to peculiar historical and economic circumstances and to many other limitations, such as the problem of communication, the older generation faced a situation in Guyana which prompted its members to involve themselves immediately in the primary task of their rehabilitation in the colony. The founding of Crabwood Creek in itself symbolizes the attempt of the older generation in this direction. The major concern of the older generation was the establishment of the group in the new setting and the arrangement of social relationships among its members. Thus under the overwhelming pressures due to social and economic rehabilitation, the members of the older generation turned inward (to their own community) rather than outward, to resolve their common problems. Mutual cooperation and the maintenance of common solidarity were the expedient rules that guided their behavior. The pattern of interaction among the people of this older generation reflects an attempt to duplicate the original patterns of Indian society, and to demonstrate their "Indianness" with as much accuracy as possible to the members of their own group. They tended to hold strongly to their past traditions and tried to replicate as nearly as possible the traditional Indian practices, the knowledge of which was a part of their shared memory. To be Indian in the true sense was of great value to this group and consequently their mode of adaptation became the recreation of their past social and cultural universe and the reassembling of their splintered cultural tradition. The older generation thus reflects the sense of ethnicity. It was not possible for the older generation to rebuild the traditional social order on the original pattern of the caste system; however, the Brahmin priesthood was necessary to legitimize their whole way of life. Thus despite the breakup of the old social order the Brahmin priesthood was retained although a new definition was given to it by the society. Under the new definition birth and ritual purity, traditionally the essentials of a Brahmin, became only secondary qualities. The evaluation of one's Karma (deeds) and his knowledge of Dharma (religious tradition) came to assume primary importance. The concepts of Dharma and Karma, the forms and functions of the family, the rituals and ceremonies connected with the rites of passage, the love for land, the agriculture based economy, and the sanctity of the cow, have survived in the older generation because these cultural items provide a basis for their ethnicity. It has been noted that certain outstanding traits of Indian culture such as the family structure, the status of the father in the family, the position of the female in the society, the segregation of males and females, the ascription of status on the basis of age, sex and kinship, and above all the ethical system based on the principles of non-violence, spiritualism, sacrifice, charity, emphasis on right means for right goals, self-discipline and thrift became the early bases of the re-formation of the East Indian society in Guyana. These cultural contents helped the group of East Indians in Guyana to retain their "Indianness." Thus the sense of ethnicity among the older generation of East Indians became a basis of their cultural continuity, and provided them with group cohesion, distinctiveness and identity.

Once the problems of rehabilitation were eased, either with the help of administrative machinery or through the medium of self-invented devices, and once the flow of fresh immigrants was stopped, the life style of the East Indian community exhibited a swing in a different direction. This was made manifest at the levels of the third and fourth generations, a category which has been called, for the purpose of this analysis, the younger generation. The changes in this category of East Indians are well pronounced. The younger generation went through a different kind of experience in the process of its adjustment and adaptation to the local environment. In their turn this generation faced a situation in which the process of intra-group interaction had almost swept away the relative isolation of the East Indian ethnic group. Market places, schools, business enterprises, political parties, recreational areas, and sugar estate sponsored community centers became focal centers where East Indians met with the members of other ethnic or racial stocks in a more than casual manner. Thus the younger generation, as opposed to the older generation, turned outward (to other cultural segments) rather than inward to resolve its problems. This turning outward also occasioned a departure from strict Indian traditional practices to a new adaptive mode which emerged as a result of the shift of reference. The constant interaction with members of other ethnic groups introduced many internal changes in the East Indian socio-cultural system. It has been noted that the younger generation demonstrates its willingness to follow the forms of tradition on various ritualistic occasions, but as observed in the preceding chapters, its members do not appear Indian in the traditional-ritualistc sense of the older generation. Their areas of immediate interest are secular and non-traditional, such as involvement in local politics, competition with others in different professions and occupations, and concern for the status of the East Indian group vis-a-vis the other ethnic groups of Guyanese society. It matters little to members of the younger generation whether they are Indian in the authentic traditional-ritualistic sense. As was observed through the mode of their participation in different rituals and ceremonies and through their reinterpretation of various traditions, their commitment to Indian tradition is mostly symbolic. What they wish is to put the East Indians in the best possible light with regard to others. The younger generation is thus Indian only in the sense that it wishes to demonstrate its Indianness to the people of other cultural groups. Their Indianness is more or less decorative rather than real for it serves to provide them a distinct group identity in the Guyanese society. To retain their ethnic character is a matter of importance for the group because it gives them a basis to validate their claim to privilege in the society by maintaining the distinctiveness and identity of the group in order to achieve the power and intrinsic rewards which result from group cohesion. Thus even when the younger generation is receptive to changes that stem from the contact situation, this does not imply that the changes are accepted at the cost of losing the ethnic identity of the East Indian group. Old cultural forms and symbols, and some of the basic cultural contents seem to have been retained with a view to establishing an identifiable position and to defining the place of the group in the society. Consequently, at the younger generational level, the sense of ethnic identity explains the basis of cultural continuities among the East Indians in Crabwood Creek.

Thus while various East Indian cultural forms and institutions may be observed to have persisted over the entire period of East Indian social existence in Guyana, observation of such forms at the generational levels reveals that even when the cultural forms have remained the same, they carry different meanings for each generational category. This differential interpretation of cultural forms is reflected in the general life style and in the nature of the group of the East Indians in Crabwood Creek. For example, we have noted a shift from the old form of arranged marriage to marriage by choice. The younger generation's attitude in this area is diametrically opposed to the attitude held by the older generation. A change has occurred, but it would appear that because of the younger generation's desire to retain ethnic identity this change has been worked out in such a manner that the hierarchy of status in the family has remained unaltered. Furthermore while we notice that the traditional system of caste endogamy is no longer practiced, this change has not resulted in the acceptance of inter-racial marriages. The strong sense of ethnic identity in the younger generation would appear to be a major factor in the transformation of the traditional concept of caste endogamy from marriage within caste to marriage within the East Indian community. Thus although the caste system became inoperative as the basis of social structure in the East Indian community, the ideology of the caste system was retained to serve as a viable basis of ethnic identity for the group.

It has been demonstrated that the ritual participation of the group's members reflects two different sets of attitudes, each representing a generational category. What is held to be sacred for one generation is purely secular for the other. It may be recalled that during marriage ceremonies while the older generation exhibited deep respect for the sanctity of the events, the younger generation celebrated the occasion in the Creole fashion by holding drinking parties, playing cards, and performing suggestive dances. Nevertheless, the differential participation which demonstrates change in the meaning and function of the cultural event at the level of the younger generation does not show itself in the actual event. It has been noted by the investigator that in all the marriages, the couples involved, although they belonged to the younger generation, went dutifully through the endless chain of traditional rituals wearing the traditional East Indian dress. They participated in all the ceremonies heavy with spiritual overtones, and when the rituals were over, the bride and groom changed from their traditional attire to a typical European style wedding gown and veil, and a full suit, respectively, and walked out of the house hand in hand as if they saluted the old and welcomed the new without disrupting either.

We will close our study with the narrative of a meaningful event. During the period of my work, the Skeldon Lions Club organized a moonlight cruise on a large ferryboat in order to raise funds for the construction of a clock tower in the Skeldon area. The announcement of the event was received with excitement in the village. About three hundred persons from all over the Corentyne area attended the event, and all ethnic and racial groups were represented. Many persons from the village were in the group including members of both of the generational categories. The boat was loaded with alcoholic beverages and left the stelling about eight o'clock at night. By ten o'clock the boat was in the middle of the river, a gentle wind was blowing in from the Atlantic, and the moon was spreading its soft light over the whole scene. Two bands started playing music, one at each end of the boat. The band on one end played the enchanting tunes of calypso music, while the band on the opposite end played lilting music from Indian films. The participants spontaneously formed two clusters. These two clusters were marked by their racial complexion. One was comprised predominantly of Negroes, and the other exclusively of East Indians. The Negro dominated cluster was mixed with boys and girls in almost equal proportion, whereas the East Indian cluster was comprised of boys with a few girls forming a separate group of their own within the cluster. The members of the older generation, almost all of them East Indians, including some ladies, stayed in the middle in a cabin overlooking the "high seas." Members of the younger generations started drinking and dancing at both ends of the boat.

On two occasions some Negro boys attempted to join the gathering at the opposite end. The reactions of the East Indian youths were immediate and sharp. They asked the Negro boys to go back to their own side. Once when a Negro youth insisted on staying on the East Indian side, the situation became so tense that the management had to intercede and ask the Negro youth to go back to his own side. Both groups continued to dance and drink. The behavior at both ends of the boat was almost identical with the exception that the girls on the East Indian side did not join in the dancing and drinking. However, some of the girls sang Indian film songs. An "emcee" in the East Indian group introduced these girl singers as the "Lata Mangeshkar" or "Asha Bhonsley" of Guyana.[1] In both groups dancing and drinking was done and sexual overtures to the members of the opposite sex were made, and yet the racial complexion of their respective clusters was maintained. When the bar ran out of drinks around three o'clock in the morning, the boat was brought back to the stelling and the participants went their separate ways. While I was descending from the boat, a young East Indian man rushed up to me and inquired with excitement, "do you likem awe (our) Hindustani music? A this na the way they do

---

[1] Lata Mangeshkar and Asha Bhonsley are the two most popular playback singers in Indian films.

in India too?" From the way he put the questions I could easily guess that the young man was expecting more of an affirmation of his ideas than an answer to his questions. It was obvious that for the questioner the Indian music carried the meaning of Indianness and thus of the ethnic identity of East Indians in Guyana. Walking with the crowd a few yards further down the road from the stelling, I met an elderly lady from Crabwood Creek who commented helplessly, "see Bhaiya awe young men have lost all awe (our) culture." To this concerned elderly lady, the dancing and drinking behavior of the East Indian youth was perceived as the loss of the old culture.

The little cruise thus provided a stage for ethnic interaction in which both the forces of tradition and of change were symbolized in the differential behavior and attitudes of the two generations. This affirms the hypothesis of this study that under the pressure of the vehement and persuasive forces of change, cultural contents and forms may be retained to serve as symbols of ethnic identity, but that the more important aspects of culture, the intrinsic meanings and functions of the forms, change selectively to permit adjustment of culture to the emerging patterns of the society.

# REFERENCES

Adams, R. N.
    1960   "An Enquiry into the Nature of the Family." Essays in the Science of Culture. Edited by Gertrude E. Dole and Robert L. Carneiro. New York: Thomas Crowell Company.

Anonymous.
    n.d.   Man-Power Citizen's Association's Foundation Souvenir (1936-39). Georgetown.

Beattie, J. H. M.
    1959   "Understanding and Explanation in Social Anthropology." The British Journal of Sociology 10: 45-60.

Beckwith, Martha B.
    1929   Black Roadways: A Study of Jamaica Folk Life. Chapel Hill: University of North Carolina Press.

Beidelman, Thomas O.
    1959   A Comparative Analysis of the Jajmani System. Association for Asian Studies. Locust Valley, New York: J. J. Augustin.

Berreman, Gerald D.
    1967   "Caste as Social Process." Southwestern Journal of Anthropology 23: 351-370.

Bidney, David
    1954   Theoretical Anthropology. New York: Columbia University Press.

Bohannan, Paul
    1963   Social Anthropology. New York: Holt, Rinehart, and Winston.

Braithwaite, Lloyd
    1960   "The Present Status of the Social Sciences in the British Caribbean." Caribbean Studies: A Symposium. Vera Rubin. Ed. Seattle: University of Washington Press.

British Guiana. Census
    1965   Census of the Colony of British Guiana, 1960. Kingston, Jamaica.

British Guiana. Commission of Inquiry
    1965   Report of the British Guiana Commission of Inquiry. Georgetown.

British Guiana. Registrar General.
    1959   The Annual Report of the Registrar General. Georgetown.

Brown, W. Norman
    1961   "The Contents of Cultural Continuity in Asia." Journal of Asian Studies 20: 427-34.

Brown, W. Norman
    1966   Man in the Universe: Some Cultural Continuities in India. Los Angeles and Berkeley: University of California Press.

Bryce-Laporte, R. S.
    1967   "M. G. Smith's Version of Pluralism—The Questions It Raises." Comparative Studies in Society and History 10: 114-20.

Clarke, Colin
    1967   "Caste Among Hindus in a Town in Trinidad: San Fernando." in Barton M. Schwartz (ed.), Caste in Overseas Indian Communities. San Francisco: Chandler Publishing Company.

Clarke, Edith
    1953   "Land Tenure and the Family in Four Communities in Jamaica." Social and Economic Studies I, no. 4: 81-117.

Clementi, Sir Cecil
    1937   A Constitutional History of British Guiana. London: MacMillan and Co., Ltd.

Cohen, Yehudi A.
    1954   "The Social Organization of a Selected Community in Jamaica." Social and Economic Studies II, no. 4. Jamaica: University College of West Indies.

1956 "Structure and Function: Family Organization and Socialization in a Jamaican Community." American Anthropologist 58: 664-86.

Dalton, Henry G.
1855 The History of British Guiana. London: Longman, Brown, Green and Longmans.

Davenport, W.
1961 "The Family System of Jamaica." Journal of Social and Economic Studies 10: 420-54.

Despres, Leo A.
1964 "The Implications of Nationalist Politics in British Guiana for the Development of Cultural Theory." American Anthropologist 66: 1051-77.
1967 Cultural Pluralism and National Politics in British Guiana. Chicago: Rand McNally and Co.
1968 "Anthropological Theory, Cultural Pluralism, and the Study of Complex Societies." Current Anthropology 9: 3-26.

Dube, S. C.
1955 Indian Village. Ithaca, New York: Cornell University Press.
1963 "A Deccan Village." in M. N. Srinivas (ed.), India's Villages. Bombay: Asia Publishing House.

Dubois, Abbe J.
1879 A Description of the People of India. (Reprint) Madras.

Durkheim, Emile
1965 The Elementary Forms of the Religious Life. New York: The Free Press.
1966 The Division of Labor in Society. New York: The Free Press.

Dutt, Romesh Chunder
1916 The Economic History of Indian in the Victorian Age From the Accession of Queen Victoria in 1837 to the Commencement of the Twentieth Century. (4th Edition) London: Kegan Paul, Trench Trubner and Co.

Fortes, Meyer
1962 "Introduction" The Developmental Cycle in Domestic Groups. Cambridge Papers in Social Anthropology, No. 1. Cambridge: Cambridge University Press.

Furnivall, J. S.
1944 Netherlands India: A Study of Plural Economy. New York: MacMillan and Co.
1948 Colonial Policy and Practice. Cambridge: Cambridge University Press.

Ghurye, G. S.
1932 Caste and Race in India. London: K. Paul, Trench Trubner and Co., Ltd.

Gough, Kathleen
1959 "The Nayars and the Definition of Marriage." Journal of the Royal Anthropological Institute 89: 23-24.

Gravesande, Laurens Storm Van 's
1911 The Rise of British Guiana. Compiled from dispatches by C. A. Harris and J. A. J. de Villiers. London: Hakluyt Society. 2 vols. (Hakluyt Society, Nos. 26-27.)

Heimsath, Charles H.
1964 Indian Nationalism and Hindu Social Reform. New Jersey: Princeton University Press.

Herskovits, M. J.
1937 Life in a Haitian Village. New York: Alfred A. Knopf.
1960 "The Ahistorical Approach to Afroamerican Studies: A Critique." American Anthropologist 62: 559-67.

Herskovits, M. J. and Frances, S.
1934 Rebel Destiny. New York: McGraw Hill Book Co., Inc.
1947 Trinidad Village. New York: Alfred A. Knopf.

Hickerson, Harold
1954 Social and Economic Organization in a Guyanese Village. Unpublished dissertation. Bloomington: Indiana University.

Holland, W. G.
    1907   Indian Review 8 (July): 7.
Hutton, J. H.
    1951   Caste in India: Its Nature, Function and Origin. Oxford: Oxford University Press (second edition).
Ishwaran, K.
    1966   Tradition and Economy in Village India. London: Routledge and Kegan Paul.
Jagan, C. B.
    1967   The West on Trial: My Fight for Guyana's Freedom. New York: International Publishers Associates.
Jayawardena, Chandra
    1963   Conflict and Solidarity in a Guyanese Plantation. London: University of London, Athlone Press.
Keesing, Felix M.
    1963   Cultural Anthropology. New York: Holt, Rinehart and Winston.
Kerr, M.
    1952   Personality and Conflict in Jamaica. Liverpool: University of Liverpool Press.
    1955   "The Study of Personality Deprivation Through Projection Tests." Social and Economic Studies IV, no. 1. Jamaica: University College of West Indies.
Kroeber, A. L.
    1948   Anthropology. New York: Harcourt, Brace and World, Inc.
Kroeber, A. L. and Clyde Kluckhohn
    1963   Culture: A Critical Review of Concepts and Definitions. New York: Vintage Books.
Kuhn, Thomas S.
    1966   The Structure of Scientific Revolutions. Chicago: Phoenix Books, University of Chicago Press.
Kuper, Hilda
    1960   Indian People in Natal. Natal: Natal University Press.
Levy, M. J., Jr. and L. A. Fallers
    1959   "The Family: Some Comparative Considerations." American Anthropologist 61: 647-51.
Lewis, Oscar
    1958   Village Life in Northern India. Urbana, Illinois: University of Illinois.
Linton, Ralph
    1960   "A Neglected Aspect of Social Organization." The American Journal of Sociology 45: 870-86.
Lounsbury, F. G.
    1965   "Another View of Trobriand Kinship Categories." in E. A. Hammel (ed.), Formal Semantic Analysis. Menasha: American Anthropologist, Special Publication 67: 142-85.
Lyall, Sir Alfred
    1889   Religious Systems of the World. London.
Marshall, A. H.
    1955   Report on Local Government in British Guiana. Georgetown. Argosy.
Ministry of Local Government. Report
    1956   "Community Development Program." Report of the Ministry of Local Government, Social Welfare and Cooperative Development. Georgetown. April 1956.
Morris, H. S.
    1968   The Indians in Uganda: A Study of Caste and Sect in a Plural Society. Chicago: University of Chicago Press.
Murdock, G. P.
    1949   Social Structure. New York: MacMillan and Co.
Nath, Dwarka
    1960   History of the Indian in British Guiana. London and New York: Nelson.
Newman, Peter
    1964   British Guiana: Problems of Cohesion in an Immigrant Society. London: Oxford University Press.

Pitts, Jesse R.
  1961 "Introduction" in Talcott Parsons, Edward Shils, Kaspar D. Naegele, and Jesse R. Pitts (eds.), Theories of Society. New York: Free Press of Glencoe.
Prabhu, Pandharinath H.
  1958 Hindu Social Organization: A Study in Socio-Psychological and Ideological Foundations. Bombay: Popular Book Depot (third edition).
Proceedings. All Indian Colloquium
  1967 All Indian Colloquium on Ethical and Spiritual Values as the Basis of National Integration. Bombay: Bharatya Vidya Bhavan.
Radcliffe-Brown
  1935 "On the Concept of Function in Social Science." American Anthropologist 37: 394-401.
Ragatz, L. J.
  1963 The Fall of the Planter Class in the British Caribbean—1763-1833. New York: Octagon Books, Inc.
Rangachari, K.
  1924 "Gotra and Pravara." Proceedings and Transactions of the Third Oriental Conference. Madras.
Redfield, Robert
  1940 "The Folk Society and Culture." American Journal of Sociology 45: 731-42.
  1947 "The Folk Society." American Journal of Sociology 52: 293-308.
Rex, J.
  1959 "The Plural Society in Sociological Theory." British Journal of Sociology 10: 114-24.
Roberts, G. W.
  1948 "Some Observations on the Population of British Guiana." Population Studies II, no. 2.
  1964 British Guiana: Problems of Cohesion in an Immigrant Society. London: Oxford University Press.
Rodway, James
  1891 History of British Guiana from the Year 1668 to the Present. London: T. F. Unwin.
Rubin, Vera, (ed.)
  1960a Caribbean Studies: A Symposium. Institute of Social and Economic Research, University College of the West Indies, 1957. Reprinted, Seattle: University of Washington Press.
  1960b "Social and Cultural Pluralism in the Caribbean." Annals of the New York Academy of Sciences 83: 761-916.
Schwartz, Barton M.
  1967 "The Failure of Caste in Trinidad" in Barton M. Schwartz (ed.), Caste in Overseas Communities. San Francisco: Chandler Publishing Co.
Simey, I. S.
  1946 Welfare and Planning in West Indies. London: Oxford University Press.
Singer, Milton
  1955 "The Cultural Pattern of Indian Civilization: A Preliminary Report of a Methodological Field Study." The Far Eastern Quarterly 15: 23-36.
Skinner, E. P.
  1955 Ethnic Interaction in a British Guiana Rural Community: A Study in Secondary Acculturation and Group Dynamics. Unpublished dissertation. New York: Columbia University.
Smith, M. G.
  1960 "The African Heritage in the Caribbean" in Vera Rubin (ed.), Caribbean Studies: A Symposium. Seattle: University of Washington Press.
  1962 West Indian Family Structure. Seattle: University of Washington Press.
  1965a The Plural Society in the British West Indies. Berkeley: University of California Press.
  1965b Stratification in Grenada. Berkeley and Los Angeles: University of California Press.

Smith, Raymond T.
  1957  "The Family in the Caribbean" in Vera Rubin (ed.), Caribbean Studies: A Symposium. Jamaica: University College of the West Indies.
  1961  Review of "Social and Cultural Pluralism in the Caribbean." Annals of the New York Academy of Sciences, Vol. 83. American Anthropologist 63: 155-57.
  1962  British Guiana. Oxford University Press for Royal Institute of International Affairs.
  1966  "People and Change" in George Lamming and Martin Carter (eds.), New World —Guyana Independence Issue. Georgetown: New World Associates.
Smith, Raymond T. and Chandra Jayawardena
  1967  "Caste and Social Status Among the Indians of Guyana" in Barton M. Schwartz (ed.), Caste in Overseas Indian Communities. San Francisco: Chandler Publishing Co.
Srinivas, M. N.
  1956  "A Note on Sanskritization and Westernization." The Far Eastern Quarterly 15: 481-96.
Srinivas, M. N. (ed.)
  1963  India's Villages. (Second revised edition.) Bombay: Asia Publishing House.
Steward, Julian H.
  1950  Area Research: Theory and Practice. New York: Social Science Research Council, Bulletin 63.
Steward, J. H., Manners, R. A., Wolf, E. R., Sedna, E. P., Mintz, S. W. and Scheck, R. L.
  1956  People of Puerto Rico. Urbana: University of Illinois Press.
Sundaram, Lanka
  1933  Indian Overseas: A Study in Economic Sociology. Madras: G. A. Natesan and Co.
Swan, Michael
  1957  British Guiana: The Land of Six Peoples. London: Her Majesty's Stationery Office.
Wagley, Charles
  1960  "Plantation America: A Culture Sphere" in Vera Rubin (ed.), Caribbean Studies: A Symposium. Seattle: University of Washington Press.
Wagley, Charles, and Harris M.
  1955  "A Typology of Latin American Subcultures." American Anthropologist 57: 428-51.
Wallbank, T. Walter, and Taylor, Lastair M. (eds.)
  1961  Civilization Past and Present, Vol. II. Chicago: Scott, Foresman and Co.
Weber, A. R.
  1931  A Centenary History and Handbook of British Guiana. Georgetown.
Yinger, Milton
  1957  Religion, Society and the Individual, Part I. New York: MacMillan and Co.

# INDEX

Abolition: Act of, 3, 23, 31; of slave trade, 23
Acculturation, XIII
Agni, 82, 85, 86, 89, 90, 92
Agnihotra, 84, 90
Agriculture, 66
American Association for the Advancement of Science, 1
Amerindians, 34, 35
Animal Husbandry 67, 68
Anti–Corn Law League, 28
Apan Jaat, 105
Arti, 85
Arya Samaj, 97; differences with Sanatan Dharma, 98, 99
Auckland, Lord, 26
Badai, 88, 93
Baryat, 85
Bastra, 86
Batenburg, Van, 41
Beattie, J. H. M., cited, 9
Beckwith, M., cited 8, 9
Beidelman, Thomas, cited 83, 95
Berbice Association, 21
Berbice County, 5, 22, 38, 41, 69
Berreman, Gerald, cited, 3, 94
Bhagavad Gita, 75
Bhanwar, 86, 90, 92
Bhaskarananda, Professor, 98
Bhuta–Yajna, 77
Bohanna, P., cited, 59
Bookers, 31
Brahama–Yajna, 77, 78
Brahma, 98
Brahman, 53, 75, 93–96, 98, 107
Braithwaite, L., cited, 10, 13, 15, 16
British East India Company, 29
Brougham, Lord, 23
Brown, N., cited, 3
Bryce–Laporte, R. S., cited, 11
Buxton, Thomas Fowell, 23
Canadian Mission School, 52, 57, 100
Caribbean Area, 1, 8; differences in social, economic and political systems of, 8; multi–racial society of, 8, 20–31
Caribbean Studies: Symposium on, 1; ethnohistorical approach, 8; acculturation studies, 8, 9; psychological approach, 9; areal and cultural evolutionary approach, 9; structural–functional framework, 9; plural society mode, 10–16, 19; unitary or consensual model, 16–17, 19; major research problems in, 8–19, 104
Carriacou, 12
Caste system, XI, 3, 26, 81, 93–96, 99, 109; caste identification, 81, 96; caste status, 95, 96; caste reinterpretation, 82, 95, 96; caste as ideology, 94, 109; caste as basis of social stratification, 94; inter–caste marriage, 95, 96
Chekai, 84, 90, 91
Chinese: Immigration of, 25, 27; population of, 34, 36, 37; movement to cities, 27, 28; Hopetown settlement of, 28
Christian Indians, 97, 100, 101
Clarke, Colin, cited, 94
Clarke, E., cited, 9
Clementi, Sir Cecil, cited, 27, 41n
Cohen, Y., cited, 9
Comins, D. W. D., cited, 100, 101
Continuity-in-change model, X
Coolies, 26, 45
Corentyne River, 41, 42, 51, 67, 75
Cow, 68, 107
Crabwood Creek: Selection for study, 5, 48–50; location of, 41–42; growth and formation of, 45–48; population of, 50–51; houses in, 57–59; households in, 59–63.
Creole culture, 63, 64, 89, 93, 109
Cultural adaptation, IX, 77, 79
Cultural continuity and change, 3, 19, 55–56, 78, 79, 83, 104, 106
Cultural forms, 78, 97, 105–106, 109
Cultural pluralism IX, XII
Cultural survival, IX, 78, 83
Cultural tradition: East Indian, 75, 77
Dairy farming, 67
Dalton, Henry G. quoted, 22; cited, 27
Dayanand Saraswati, 98
Demarara, 26, 38
Despres, Leo: cited, 8–9, 11, 15–16, 46n
Deva–Yajna, 77, 78
Dharma–riti, 84, 89, 90
Dharmasastras, 81, 82
Dholak, 91
Dispersed village, 75
"Doghula", 50
Doolha Pooja, 86
Drainage and irrigation, 30, 32, 57, 72
Dube, S. C., cited, 47, 64
Durkheim, E., 9, 10, 11, 13, 16
Dutch Company, 21
Dutt, Romesh Chunder, cited, 29

Dwar–Pooja, 85
East Indians: population in Guyana, 1, 35–38; population in Crabwood Creek, 51 (tab.); as indentured labor, 2, 25–27; replacement of Negro slaves, 2; as field labor, 2, 25–26; placement in rural areas, 2, 5, 36; generational attitudes of, X, 7, 17–19, 50–53, 70, 81–84, 88–93, 95–96, 107–108; religion of, 97–103; religious festivals of, 103
El Dorado, 20
"Engenho", 21
Essequibo, 30, 38, 50, 70
Ethnic conflict, XII, 53, 110
Ethnic groups: definition, 106; East Indian, 35, 37; Negroes, 36–37; Chinese, 36–37; Portuguese, 36–37; Europeans, 37
Ethnic identity, 19, 53, 101, 106, 108, 109, 111; definition of, 107
Ethnic population (Crabwood Creek), 51 (tab.)
Ethnic, XII; definition of, 106
Exogamy, 81–82, 94
"Factory labor", 2
Family, 77–79, 102, 109; traditions, 84, 87
Female dress, 63–65; social status, 77
Female labor, 67, 69, 70, 72
"Field Labor", 2
Fishing, 67
Fortes, Meyer, cited, 61
Frederici, Governor, 41
Furnivall, J. S.: cited, 10, 11, 12; quoted, 11;
  plural society concept of, 11, 12
Gandhi, Mahatma, 29, 64
Ganesh, 85, 89, 90
Ganges, 88
Gaon–riti, 84, 87, 88
Gauri, 85, 89
Gautama–Dharmasutra, 82
Georgetown, 20, 23, 41, 45, 49, 53
Ghurye, G. S., 92n
Gift exchange, 84, 85, 86, 89, 90, 91
Gladstone, John, 25
Gotra, 82, 82n
Gravesande, Laurens Storm Van's, 21
Grenada, 12
Guyana; 20–21; British occupation, 23, 31, 41; area, 32; people, 35; climate, 33–34; geographical divisions, 32–33; administrative structure, 38–40.
Hardi, 85
Harikatha, 95–96, 102
Hausa, 12
Heimsath, Charles, cited, 98–99

Herskovits, M. J., 8
Herskovits, M. J., and F. S.: cited, 8; ethnohistorical approach of, 8
Hesperus, 26
Hickerson, Harold, cited, 27
Hindus, 55, 88–90, 92, 94, 96–99, 102–103
Holland, W. G., cited, 99
Hopetown, 28
Household Heirarchy, 61–63
Households, 59–61; types of, 59; number of persons by types, 60 (tab.)
Houses, 57–59; number of rooms in, 60 (tab.)
Houses: as source of prestige, 58–59
Hutton, J. H.: cited, 3
Hypergamy, 94, 95
Hypogamy, 94, 95
Immigration, 35; of labor, 25–28; indentured, 25–29, 35–38; termination of indentured labor, 29, 51; Agent–General, 35, 50; Registrar General, 35, 38, 50
Indian Cultural Council, 103
Indian Culture, IX, X, 76, 77
Indianness, 106–108, 111
Ishwaran, K., cited IX, quoted, 89
Jagan, Chedi B., 5, 6, 25
Jahazi Bhai, 54
Jajmani system, 83, 95
Jama, 85, 87, 93
Jamaica, 12
Janwas, 85
Jati, 93, 94, 95, 96
Jayamuni, Mehta, 98
Kadara (Nigeria), 12
Kagora, 12
Kakan, 88
Kali Puja, 50, 68, 75
Kanya–Dana, 81, 86, 90, 92
Karma, 99, 107
Kenya, 14
Keesing, F. M., cited, 9, 13
Kerr, M., cited, 9
Khoka, 32, 33, 48, 49, 72
Kroeber, A. L., quoted, 18, 19
Kuli–riti, 84, 87, 89
Kumar–Patra, 85
Kuper, Hilda, cited, 94
Lakshmi, 85
Lava Havan, 86, 90, 92
Lethem, Sir Gordon, Governor, 48
Levy, M. J. and L. A. Fallers, cited, 78
Linton, Ralph, cited, 76
Logging, 33, 49, 54, 62, 68–69
Lounsbury, F. G., cited, 78
Lyall, Sir Alfred, cited, 97
Madhu Parka, 86

Mahabharata, 53, 77n, 78n
Malinowski, B.: cited, 9; structure-functionalism of, 9, 10
Manava Grihyasutra, 82
Manushya-Yajna, 77
Manusimirti, 77, 81
Maraj, Ramnauth, 46
Marriage, 79-93, 100
Marshall, A. H., cited, 40
Marua (Nuptial Pole), 85, 86, 87, 88, 90, 91, 92
Mati-Kore, 84, 85, 91
Melting pot model, IX
Miaji, 55
Milap, 85
Morris, H. S., cited, 105
Murdock, G. P., cited, 78
Murti, Pooja, 98
Muslims, 55, 68, 96, 99, 100, 101, 102, 103
Naichu (Nichawar), 85, 86
Naido, Sarojini, 64
Nath, D., cited, 25n, 26, 36, 81, 82
Nawa, 83, 85, 95
Negroes: percentage in Guyana population, 35-37; as ethnic group, 1, 2, 36-37; workers as task force, 2; as factory labor, 2; reluctance to work on land, 2
New Amsterdam, 39, 45, 49, 50
Newman, Peter, cited, 37
Nigeria, 14
Nucleated village, 75
Oriental College, Guyana, 98
Pandit, 83-92, 96; duties of, 92, 95; authority of, 91, 95; council of, 95
Parchay, 85
Parivar, 82
Parsons, T: cited, XI, 11, 13; Action Theory of, 11, 16
Pat-Mauri, 85, 88, 93
Patroons, 20, 21
Peere, Van, 20n
Pershad, Ayudhya, 98
Phagwa, 55
Pitri, 102
Pitri-Yajna, 77-78
Planters: British, 21-22; resources and work of, 30-31; image of, 23-24; reaction to abolition of slavery, 25
Plural society model, XI, XII; foundation of, 11-17, 31, 104
Prabhu, P. H., cited, 82
Putra, 102
Quran Parhey, 55, 100
Racial growth of population, 37 (tab.)
Racial population distribution, 37 (tab.)

Radcliffe-Brown: cited, 9, 10; structure-functionalism of, 9, 10
Ragatz, L. J.: cited, 23n; quoted, 23
Raksha Bandhan, 103
Raleigh, Sir Walter, 20
Ramayana, 53
Rangachari, K., 82n
Redfield, R.: cited, 9, 76
Rice: cultivation of, 46, 59; annual cycle of production, 71; single crop system, 71-74; ploughing, 72; watering, 72; drying, 72; reaping, 72-73; expenditure and income in production, 74
Rigveda, 77n
Roberts, G. W., cited, 36, 36n, 37
Rodway, James: quoted, 23, 26, cited, 24, 25
Rubin, Vera, cited, 1, 10, 11, 15
Sanatan Dharm, 97; Maha Sabha, 97-98; differences with Arya Samaj, 98, 99
Sapinda, 82
Sat-Bachan, 86, 87
Satya-Narain Katha, 85
Sawmilling, 66, 68-69
Schwartz, Barton, cited, 94
Sendoor (Red ochre), 87
Shiva, 98
Sierra Leone, 27
Simey, T., cited, 9
Singer, M., cited, 3
Skeldon Sugar Factory, 41, 46, 47, 50, 66, 68, 69, 110
Skinner, E. P., cited, 25, 70, 103
Slave trade, 22; abolition of, 2, 12, 23-24, 28, 31; Anti-Slavery Bill, 23; Anti-Slavery Movement, 23
Slaves: compensation for loss, 24n; reaction to emancipation, 24; establishment of cooperative villages, 24; emancipation and sugar industry, 24-25
Smith, E. M. L., quoted, 26
Smith, John (Martyr Smith), 23
Smith, M. G.: cited, IX, XI, 1, 8, 10-12, 35; quoted, 10, 12, 15; plural society model of, 11-16; analysis of plural society model of, 16, 17; catagories of institutions, 14; improvement over Furnivall's model, 12-15
Smith, R. T.: cited, 10, 13, 16, 17, 20n, 21; unitary or consensual model of, 16
Smith, R. T. & Jayawardena C., cited, 81n, 94
Social institutions; catagories of, 14
Society: classification of, 14
South Africa, Union of, 12, 14
Spouse selection, 79-81
Srinivas, M.: cited, 3

Steward, J.: cited, 9; areal and cultural evolutionary approach of, 9
Sugar industry: labor problems in, 24–28, 31; participation in administration, 39
Sugar plantations: growth & development, 21, 22
Surinam, 41
Swan, M., cited, 22; quoted, 22
"Tasks", 69
Tilak, 84, 90, 91
Transportation, 69
Unitary or Consensual Model, 16, 17, 104
University of Puerto Rico, 1
University College of the West Indies, 1
"Usina", 22

Van Batenburg, Governor, 41
Varna, 93, 94, 95, 96, 99
Varuna, 85, 89
Vedas, 75, 84, 99
Vishnu, 98
Vivah, 86, 90, 92
Wagley, C: cited, 8
Weber, M., 13, 16
Weddings: rituals, 78, 82–93
Whitby, 26
Wilberforce, William, 23
Wolesely, W. B., 26
Yagya, 50, 68, 75, 102
Yinger, Milton, cited, 97